Praise for
Moving Forward

"A compassionate and very personal examination of the hows and whys of self-forgiveness. Blending the sensitivity of a counselor with the rigor of a scientist is no easy accomplishment, and that is what has made Everett Worthington the most sought-after expert on forgiveness for nearly two decades. Read this book and learn how to move forward in your own journey of self-forgiveness."

—Robert Emmons, editor-in-chief of *The Journal of Positive Psychology* and author of *Gratitude Works!* and *Thanks! How Practicing Gratitude Can Make You Happier*

"Why do we see the need to forgive others while overlooking the importance of forgiving ourselves? Everett Worthington knows from hard experience that both are necessary, but neither is easy. Now you can benefit from his years of research—as well as life-tested application—in taking the only path that will free you from shame and self-condemnation."

—Dr. Tim Clinton, president of the American Association of Christian Counselors and executive director of the Center for Counseling and Family Studies at Liberty University

"Researcher-clinician Everett Worthington, the world's leading expert on the science and practice of forgiveness, now points the way to self-forgiveness. For those of us who are painfully aware of our flaws—and that's most of us—this grace-filled book shows how to lighten the burden of self-blame and guilt, how to discover and embrace God's love, and how to experience healing."

—David G. Myers, Hope College social psychologist and author of *A Friendly Letter to Skeptics and Atheists*

"Who doesn't know the feeling of being stuck in a rut or weighed down with self-condemnation? This book is for all of us who are honest enough to confess our need to make peace with ourselves. Dr. Worthington has suffered through darkness and now uses the story of his personal pain to light the way for all of us. Read *Moving Forward* and join him on the inspiring journey of self-forgiveness and true peace."

—Les Parrott, PhD, author of *Shoulda Coulda Woulda*

MOVING FORWARD

Six Steps to Forgiving Yourself and Breaking Free from the Past

EVERETT L. WORTHINGTON JR.

WATERBROOK
PRESS

Moving Forward

This book is not intended to replace the medical advice of a trained medical professional. Readers are advised to consult a physician or other qualified health-care professional regarding treatment of their medical problems. The author and publisher specifically disclaim liability, loss, or risk, personal or otherwise, which is incurred as a consequence, directly or indirectly, of the use or application of any of the contents of this book.

Details in some anecdotes and stories have been changed to protect the identities of the persons involved.

Trade Paperback ISBN 978-0-307-73151-7
eBook ISBN 978-0-307-73152-4

Cover design by Kristopher K. Orr; cover image by Biwa Studio, Getty Images

Published in the United States by WaterBrook, an imprint of the Crown Publishing Group, a division of Penguin Random House LLC, New York.

Library of Congress Cataloging-in-Publication Data
Worthington, Everett L., 1946–
Moving forward : six steps to forgiving yourself and breaking free from the past / Everett L. Worthington, Jr.—1st Edition.
pages cm
Includes bibliographical references.
ISBN 978-0-307-73151-7—ISBN 978-0-307-73152-4 (electronic)
1. Forgiveness—Religious aspects—Christianity. 2. Self-acceptance—Religious aspects—Christianity. 3. Regret—Religious aspects—Christianity. I. Title.
BV4647.F55W67 2013
234'.5—dc23
2013004406

Printed in the United States of America
2018

10 9 8 7 6 5 4 3

To Kirby, who modeled what it takes to break free from self-blame and shame and inspired me to learn to love God better. I don't deserve you.

To my children, the people at Christ Prez, and my friends at VCU, who have believed in me and provided needed, persistent support. I don't deserve you either.

To my colleagues, who are graduate students, professors, and counselors—and also are my friends. I cherish our mutual learning about forgiveness and virtue. There is no way I could deserve such wonderful colleagues. I am grateful that the Lord has provided abundantly.

CONTENTS

Part 3: Step 1—Receive God's Forgiveness

Part 4: Step 2—Repair Relationships

Part 5: Step 3—Rethink Ruminations

Part 6: Step 4—Reach Emotional Self-Forgiveness

A Personal Note to Get Us Started

Forgiveness is hard; we all know that. What comes as a surprise to many of us is this: forgiving yourself can be much harder still. When you are the wrongdoer who needs to be forgiven—and you are the one who needs to forgive—a struggle results that has few equals.

In *Moving Forward* you will learn research-proven steps to forgiving others and yourself. The steps also have been tear-tested in the difficulties and darkness of real life and worked through in the counseling room. As we work through the six steps in the chapters that follow, you will gain life-changing insight into your nature as a person. And you will discover a number of truths about yourself—things you might already have suspected but weren't yet prepared to take a close look at.

The truth about you (and all of us) is hard to accept, but it's powerful and life changing when you do face it and engage with it. The truth is this: you are more flawed than you can imagine. But, miraculously, you also are far more valuable and more cherished than you can imagine.

You—and everyone else—are a contrast of flaws and unspeakable value that is difficult to fathom. But when you do get it, and I finally "got it" as I moved through my own struggles, the breakthrough is a glorious shift in the way you live. So join with me to work through a process that will be much harder than you expect but will end with the freedom you have been seeking. You can live without self-blame and condemnation, without the familiar burden of guilt, and in a place where you can embrace the precious value of being a flawed person who is deeply loved by God.

The work that is required to reach self-forgiveness will seem daunting. And with good reason. It is more demanding than most of the challenges you will take on in life. But the difficult work eventually achieves a goal that few people reach. Self-forgiveness releases you from shame and self-condemnation and leads to freedom and long-lasting internal peace.

All of this begins with God's recipe for self-acceptance, which is summed up as "you are flawed, but precious." The real struggle in gaining meaningful victory over self-blame is not simply saying you are forgiving yourself. You can forgive yourself with full understanding and yet still feel just as guilty and ashamed of your misdeeds. The hardest struggle—beyond self-forgiveness—is *accepting* yourself as a flawed individual (we all are), and yet being convinced that you are precious to the Lord. You are valued more highly than you can imagine.

After you work through the steps to self-forgiveness, you will experience something that Paul came to realize in his life. Paul couldn't change his past persecution of Christians, but he knew he was living a new life. Likewise, you can admit to your past failures and the things you regret yet strain forward to the future (see Philippians 3:13).

I hope your sense of hope will be renewed as we embark on a journey that will involve a lot of work but will lead to the destination we all long for. So are you ready to work through the six steps to forgiving yourself? Here is the sneak-peek outline.

Step 1: Receive God's Forgiveness

Step 2: Repair Relationships

Step 3: Rethink Ruminations

Step 4: REACH Emotional Self-Forgiveness

Step 5: Rebuild Self-Acceptance

Step 6: Resolve to Live Virtuously

Now let's get started.

Part 1

A Life Turned Upside-Down

I Love Paris in the Summer

Our dream trip to Europe could not have been a bigger disaster

> Guilt upon the conscience, like rust upon iron, both defiles and consumes it, gnawing and creeping into it, as that does which at last eats out the very heart and substance of the metal.
>
> —Bishop Robert South

Sometimes the most innocent-seeming things can turn your life topsy-turvy. For me, it was an e-mail I received while working online at a sweltering Paris Internet café.

"Call me immediately," wrote our friend Sherry Linger. While we were in Europe, Sherry was scheduling my wife's (Kirby) speaking and travel engagements for the coming winter season. I assumed a call was needed due to something that had come up with my wife's schedule.

I jogged back to our hotel to get Kirby. But it turned out the message wasn't for her. That urgent e-mail was directed at me, and it would lead to a maelstrom of emotions. I soon would give in to seething anger at God. And eventually—after a long period of anguish—I would be able to finally confront my self-blame and shame. I would have to use my knowledge and skills as a psychologist, draw on my experience as a counselor, and wrestle with God day and night. I had no idea that my life would come to this.

Over the years I had known shame and personal guilt. I have regrets just as you do. But I never dreamed that at age fifty-eight, my entire being would engage in battle with my past failures—and one in particular that I was convinced had led to the death of someone I'd loved my entire life.

I would not rest until I could determine whether it was possible to forgive myself. It seemed my failures would overwhelm me. I was out of my depth as a psychologist and as a person of faith. The next step and the one after that were hidden in darkness, and the journey was one I had to take largely on my own. Always there was the concern that I couldn't deny: what would happen if, at the end of this struggle, I found that it was *impossible* to forgive myself?

I worked harder during this crisis than I have ever worked on any issue in my life. The struggle would weigh so heavily on me that, at times, I wondered if I could survive the process. Could I stand up under it until the issue was resolved? I made progress, very slowly and over a period of years. And then God gave me another challenge that I would have to meet. I would have to face this question: could I use my own experiences to help lessen the pain of others who have been marinating in shame and self-blame? By the end of this book, maybe you can answer that question for me—and even for yourself.

I hope this book will help you. If you struggle with self-blame resulting from something you did or should have done but didn't, or if you feel that you have not lived up to your expectations, I hope you'll break free from that guilt and self-blame. If you have a friend or loved one struggling in this regard, perhaps this book can help you help him or her.

A Different Approach to Self-Forgiveness

Moving Forward is unlike other books that are designed to help you address major problems that hold you back or drain your energy. The others tend to name the problem and then proceed immediately to a list of solutions. The struggle between self-condemnation and self-forgiveness, however, is different. It is worthy of careful examination and deep understanding. Self-blame is a personal issue that bears little resemblance to most other major life issues. The struggle is with yourself, and much of the work that needs to be done is in understanding yourself, the circumstances of your biggest regrets, and the effect of these issues on your daily life.

I will share both clinical and scientific results to help shed light on the struggle as well as on the journey toward self-forgiveness. But because self-forgiveness is so personal, I also will tell stories that describe the most difficult struggle I have ever faced. This is not to say that my experience is like most other people's or that it should be a model for the approach you will take. The value in telling my story is that it is intensely personal, like your story, and that it illustrates the long and difficult series of decisions and practical steps necessary to forgive yourself. As you read my story, interspersed with chapters that provide solid, researched, tested approaches to self-forgiveness, you will gain a more fully formed picture of all that is involved in addressing your shame, guilt, and regrets. I believe that, despite the differences between my story and yours, you will gain insight and understanding into how you can deal with self-condemnation.

As you begin to walk through your own story, you will be introduced to the six steps that led to my self-forgiveness and that have helped others to wrestle successfully with self-forgiveness. My story of failing my brother and myself, will help you think about your own life. And as I relate these stories, I will show how the Six Steps to Self-Forgiveness apply.

Even though this book is personal, the advice and solutions it offers are not simply the ideas fashioned by one person who found that they worked in his life. I am a psychologist who has studied forgiveness scientifically for more than twenty years. I have seen countless individuals and couples struggle with self-blame, led more than one hundred groups of people who are trying to forgive others and sometimes themselves, and seen lots of pain and healing expressed in those groups. I also am a person of faith. Like many people, I have experienced times of closeness to God and other times of silent distance from God. But this book tells about the largest swings in my life of faith. There were times when I came very close to losing my faith completely.

The hard path from self-condemnation to self-forgiveness is not a mountain trail laid out for people who have everything—including their spiritual life—all worked out. It is for those of us who acknowledge that much of what we face in life is too big to figure out on our own. We know our limitations, and we certainly know our pain and the longing for healing. As you read, I expect you will think: *I don't know Everett Worthington, but I am familiar with the inclines, valleys, underbrush, and cliffs in this mountain trek.* I am grateful, for our sakes, that God is a great Mountain Guide and does not let go even when we try to escape from wise counsel and loving help.

The Phone Call That Plunged Me into Darkness

If I tell my story well, it can help you apply lessons that have been life- and research-tested by many people. Those lessons open the way to overcome self-blame, unwarranted shame, and legitimate (and even false) guilt. It is natural to blame yourself for wrongs you've done or for failing to reach high enough in life—for giving up before achieving your potential. We all do that at times. I sank into the depths of guilt and self-blame while Kirby and I were in Europe.

Ironically, we were in Paris, where the early summer can be liberating. This was especially true in 2005, at the end of six years of near-constant, life-numbing pressure. Kirby and I were living for ten days in a small hotel in the north of Paris, just west of the train station, Gare du Nord, near the foot of Montmartre. We trekked several times daily to the fifth floor of a walk-up hotel room. We loved the quaint Parisian small-hotel feel, with its wrought-iron banisters and demitasse teacups. It was bare bones in terms of luxury—less than a baby-step up from a hostel. But, ah, it was Paris.

It was July, and we had entered the second week of a two-month vacation prior to my assuming a visiting research-scholar position at Cambridge University. Kirby and I planned to travel around Europe to depressurize from my six years as chair of psychology at Virginia Commonwealth University (VCU). Although I kept teaching and doing research, it was the sheer weight of people problems that had worn on me. With more than twelve hundred undergraduate psychology majors, one hundred twenty-five doctoral students, fifteen staff, and almost fifty full-time faculty, it was a rare day when no one needed my input regarding an emotional problem. I was ready for an emotionally calm period.

We arrived at London's Heathrow Airport on July 11, humped our luggage up to Cambridge University, and bused back to London with one backpack each for two months of travel in Europe. We visited our favorite spots in London and even saw (again) *Les Misérables,* one of the best stories of forgiveness ever dramatized. The protagonist, Jean Valjean, recently released from prison, steals silver and, unexpectedly, is forgiven by a priest. In turn, the thief eventually forgives Inspector Javert, the soul of relentless justice. Not only is *Les Mis* about forgiving others, it is a profound study of self-forgiveness. Javert cannot accept forgiveness and mercy from a criminal. Worse, for him, he cannot forgive himself for taking the mercy offered by Valjean.

Inspector Javert commits suicide. What's more, Valjean, the former thief who had been merciful to others, cannot forgive himself for his own failures.[1] As I sat enthralled in a dark London theater, I didn't know I was being primed for Paris.

In Paris, as we had in London, we walked from museum to museum. After a week, my shoes were broken-backed and crooked-heeled. We suffered from museum overload. So we took the day off and went to the Bois de Boulogne, a huge park similar to New York's Central Park. We strolled through shady lanes and enjoyed a respite from the mid-July heat. I was feeling very Parisian, *mais oui.*

About 2:00 p.m. we went back to the hotel. Kirby stayed in the room while I headed out to an Internet café. I sat in exotic Paris, hunched over a confusing French keyboard in a stuffy Internet café, catching up on e-mail.

In the midst of processing junk e-mail, Sherry's "call me immediately" message pinged me. I hustled to the hotel to tell Kirby, and we phoned Richmond, Virginia. I handed Kirby the phone. She said the usual "hellos," then her face fell. "Oh no," she said. She turned to me. "Your brother, Mike, committed suicide this morning."

I took the phone. "Sherry?" She told me what she knew.

I phoned Mike's wife, Charlene, who was at a police station in Tennessee. Mike had worked as an accountant in Oak Ridge.

"I can't believe it," Charlene said.

"How are you holding up?"

"Not well."

"Do you know what happened?"

"The police are investigating, but apparently he smothered himself. They said it looks like he planned this well in advance. It's probably too soon to say, but I don't think we're going to have a service."

"We can come back to be with you if it would help."

"No. We have people at church. David is devastated, of course. He can't believe his father would kill himself. But David and I will get through this. There's no sense in you and Kirby coming back—especially if there's no service. Just come and see me when you get back home."

"If you're sure—"

"We'll be fine. Listen, I have to go. The police are beckoning. So I reckon I'll be saying good-bye."

"Okay. Bye then."

"Oh, one other thing," said Charlene. (Whenever a person says "one other thing," I always think of the rumpled 1970s television police detective Columbo, played by Peter Falk. When he said "one other thing," he was about to ask the crucial question that the villain would find later was the case-busting, telltale point. In this instance, there was a disturbing similarity.)

"What's that?" I said to Charlene.

"Mike left a suicide note. The police have it. They won't tell us what's in it. Mike addressed the note not to me or to David, but to you, Ev."

2

Flashbacks to the Origins of Self-Condemnation

The solution begins with a courageous—and daunting—look to the past

Unless we remember we cannot understand.

—E. M. Forster

My brother's suicide was not the first major loss I had suffered due to violence. My introduction to the horrors of violent death came on New Year's Day 1996.

I received a call from my brother, Mike. His voice was shaky. He said, "You have to come to Tennessee. Call Kathy. Mama has been murdered."

I felt like I had been kicked in the gut. "What happened?"

"I phoned to wish her Happy New Year. She didn't answer. Because she didn't drive, I was worried. So I went over to check on her and the house was trashed."

He got choked up. When he spoke, it was in fragments. "David was with me. There was blood all over the walls. I looked down and there was her body. Beaten. Bloody. I covered David's eyes. He's only ten. There was so much blood. I phoned the police. I'm next door now. So much blood. Come today."

I phoned my sister, Kathy, and her husband, Damian, who lived not far from Kirby and me. I broke the news, and we decided they would drive to Tennessee and I would ride with them.

Over the next hour I packed and repacked my clothes. *This couldn't be,* I thought. *Who could murder a sweet, older southern woman?* I pictured my mother's soft, double-chinned face. Her gray-brown hair always seemed to be done up. And her big blue eyes peered through her glasses vulnerably. When she hugged her grandkids, they disappeared into soft grandmother, as if they were being surrounded by a comforter.

After a seven-hour drive from Richmond to Knoxville, we were suddenly drawn into a murder investigation. It was chaotic and unreal. The sweet smell of neighbor-made pies and cakes mixed with the teary salt of loss and anger. At one point, the police took Mike, Kathy, and me to the house where I spent my first twenty-two years. From the outside, it looked the same as always, except for the yellow crime-scene tape. The police detective, brusque and efficient, took us to the back door.

"The burglar entered here," he said. "He broke this window." The detective pointed to a taped and boarded section above the doorknob. "He reached in and unlocked the door. Must have started searching immediately."

We stepped across the threshold.

"Watch the flour on the floor," he warned, as if we would track through the mess. "The burglar was in a hurry. He was looking for valuables. He dumped the sugar, the flour. He pulled things from shelves. This guy has burgled houses before. He knew where people hide things."

The refrigerator, pulled away from the wall, showed a black slash-wound on its door. "That's fingerprint powder," said the detective. "We hoped for prints. No luck."

Then we turned right and stepped into a book-strewn hallway. From the corner of my eye I could see Mike pull back. It was strange to see a three-hundred-pound, six-foot-tall man recoil. He probably was reliving his first sight of Mama's crumpled body. My eyes skipped over the bookcase and landed on two drying, but still-sticky, pools of blood on the carpet. Mama's head and hips had lain in those circles as her life drained away. The burglar had bludgeoned her with a crowbar and violated her with a wine bottle.

I kept looking sidelong at the blood as we examined the debris in the living room and bedroom. We identified two things that might be missing.

Putting Together the Story

That night, Mike, Kathy, and I met in Mike's back room to piece together what we had learned. Apparently, one or two teenagers—at that point the police were not sure which—thought they could commit the burglary without being caught. My mom had gone to bed early, and there was no car sitting in the driveway beside her darkened house because she didn't drive. It looked to the intruders like the perfect setup for their crime: family gone to a New Year's party until after midnight.

She must have awakened as the youth hurled books from the bookcase in the hall. She had surprised the intruder as she came out of her bedroom. He was still holding the crowbar he had used to break the window to get into the house. He attacked her with the steel rod. Then, angered and upset, he molested her with a wine bottle as she lay bleeding.

I have told this story before in other books[1] and in talks. I moved from mind-numbing initial rage to later rumination. At first, all I wanted was revenge. *What type of monster,* I wondered, *would enter an elderly woman's house and do this? No punishment was too harsh. Other innocent citizens needed to be protected from such an animal as this.*

At first I had no interest in forgiving the young man who killed my mother. But I did forgive him. I would never have done it on my own, but in this instance my professional work benefited my personal life in a way that I desperately needed.

Finding the Way to Forgiveness

If you are like me, you have tried to achieve forgiveness on your own. You know it's the right thing to do, and you've read that refusing to forgive gives the wrongdoer power over you. You have heard sermons or talks on forgiveness, pointing out that it sets you free regardless of how the offender responds or chooses not to respond. Clearly, forgiveness is the difficult yet necessary course to take.

Few of us dispute the slogans that stress the personal benefits of forgiving others. And it would take a hardened heart to resist the inspirational stories about wronged people who finally found a way to overcome their desire for revenge by extending forgiveness. I knew intellectually that without forgiveness, we are destined to hold on to our anger and bitterness. But simply knowing it to be true and coming to a place where forgiveness makes a difference in your life are two very different things.

While it is necessary to be reminded that taking the hard path of forgiveness is beneficial to you when you are the wronged party, ultimately it is not all that helpful. It's like being told that your car's engine needs an overhaul. You know you'll be better off with a smooth-running car. But unless you're a trained mechanic with all the necessary tools close at hand, knowing your car needs an overhaul does you no good. That is one reason why my colleagues and I researched and developed the five-step approach known as REACH Forgiveness,[2] to help people take the necessary steps in forgiving those who have wronged them.

While this approach was developed in my work as a psychologist and has been supported with twenty-two published research studies around the world,[3] I found that it was valid for me *personally* as well. I worked through the five steps, just as we recommend for all who have been wronged and need to forgive.

I will develop the approach in detail in part 6 of this book, where REACH Forgiveness is applied to the more difficult task of forgiving yourself. For now, here are the five steps of REACH in summary form:

R stands for *recall the hurt.* You need to reframe the event or series of events—the pattern of having been wronged—differently from the way human nature tries to direct you. When you are hurt unjustly, your default reaction is to blame the offender and feel that you have been victimized and seriously injured.

E stands for *emotional replacement.* Unforgiveness, once it takes hold, is stubborn. It won't step aside of its own doing. It has to be replaced with a healthy, constructive, sustainable response. Working through the five steps of REACH Forgiveness can lead to empathy, sympathy, compassion, or love for the offender. I know this sounds impossible on a human level—*love* for the killer?! Yet it is something that God's grace can infuse, with the right timing and right time spent. I don't presume that I can understand it, but literally tens of thousands of people have experienced this mystery. And I was blessed to be one of those.

A stands for giving an *altruistic gift of forgiveness.* Forgiveness is not deserved, nor is it fair, which helps explain why it is so difficult. Why should the wrongdoer escape your wrath? After all, *you* are the wronged party. And why should you be denied the satisfaction of getting revenge or evening the score? This third step in the process shows you why.

C stands for *commit to the forgiveness you experience.* Memory experts tell us that once we have experienced an emotional change—such as forgiving someone who wronged us—we will hold on to that memory and live it out, but usually only if we make a big deal out of it. For instance, when Joshua led the ancient Israelites across the Jordan River into the Promised Land, the people erected a monument to commemorate what

God had done. They never wanted to forget how God had freed them from slavery and taken them to their own land. Committing to the forgiveness we experience through a public statement helps us remember. That also brings us to the last of the five steps.

H stands for *hold on to forgiveness whenever you doubt you have forgiven.* Our bodies hold on to a memory of having been hurt in the past. This helps explain why we react emotionally when we get into a situation where we were hurt previously. Emotional warnings such as anger and fear can alert us to be careful so that we won't be hurt again. But after we forgive someone, we often think that we should no longer feel negative emotions when we see the person again. That is a wrong assumption. If our bodies are working properly, we will still experience fear and anger in the presence of a forgiven offender. That is why we work hard to put in place an effective reminder of our commitment to forgive. This serves to call to mind the fact that we *have* forgiven the person.

The REACH Forgiveness program is captured in one acronym, and the letters serve as easy reminders of the five essential steps. It has worked for tens of thousands of people who have been through our research groups and many thousands of other people in churches and community groups from Singapore to Africa to Brazil. But implementing the steps is hard work. I found that it was one of the most difficult things I have ever attempted when I applied it to the challenge of forgiving my mother's murderer. But I had God's help, and God moved me though the steps.

I found forgiveness for the murderer even as I remembered my rage of that first night: "I wish whoever did this were here. I'd beat his brains out." I said this out loud in Mike's back room. But later, as I worked through the REACH Forgiveness model, forgiveness finally grabbed me in the gut. At last I thought, *Whose heart is darker here? The youth with an impulse control problem who reacted in rage at having his perfect crime interrupted, fearing he would go to jail? Or the university professor, couple coun-*

selor, Christian, and forgiveness researcher—who wanted with all his heart to beat the young man to death?

I knew the painful answer. Yet, I also knew that God had forgiven me and continues to forgive me. I thought, *If I can be forgiven my darkness of heart, then how can I not forgive this young man?*

Forgiveness is necessary, and much research shows that it is an action that leads to improved physical health.[4] But it does not take away the sadness and grief caused by the loss. I didn't experience the trauma of discovering my mother's body. Instead, I had more than eight hours to prepare before seeing her blood on the carpet. My brother, Mike, however, was deeply traumatized—though he tried to hide it.

Over the next two years I dealt with my grief. But Mike couldn't purge the sight of the body and the blood.

On one trip back to Knoxville for a visit, I drove past the house where we grew up. Another family was living there. People with their own flour jars, neatly stacked books, ordered rooms, unbroken mirrors. People who had never seen the yellow crime-scene tape choking the life out of our memories. I never drove by again.

Whenever I was in Knoxville on business, I would visit Mike and Charlene. In November 2004, almost nine years after the murder, I offered to take Mike, Charlene, and David out for our usual trip to the Chinese buffet near their home. This time, though, Charlene had a migraine and David was going to a basketball game. So Mike and I went. We had the best conversation of our adult lives.

Mike confided to me. "I have these *spells.* I get depressed. It's like a darkness covering me. I can't stand light. I picture Mama's body at the end of the hallway, and those walls covered with splattered blood. I can't do anything to help, to ease her pain or fear. It is so vivid that it feels like I'm there."

"How do you handle it?" I asked.

"Some Saturdays it gets so bad that I'll go to our bedroom, pull the shades, turn out the lights, and sit in the dark all day. After almost nine years I should be over this. But I get these spells. I know that isn't good."

I said, "Mike, it sounds like you have posttraumatic stress disorder. These are the symptoms. You might need some counseling."

He looked at me with a trembling lower lip and said, "I'm not going to any shrink." He said this, of course, to his brother the shrink.

I tried again. "Mike, if you have not gotten over these 'spells,' as you call them, in almost nine years, chances are you aren't going to get over them in another year—unless you get help."

"I am *not* going to any damned shrink. And I don't want to hear more about it."

"Well, *whatever,*" I said, like a petulant adolescent, and I didn't bring it up again. But that next summer, when Kirby and I returned the urgent phone call we received in Paris, it was my childish "whatever" that slugged me in the heart. I kicked myself for having been intimidated by Mike's emotional reaction, which had thrust me back into our adolescent conflicts as brothers.

As a clinical psychologist, I knew that in the face of his resistance I needed to retreat. I also knew that after a while I could be more persistent, if I was tactful about it. But I didn't do what I knew how to do. I let childhood patterns get in the way. In Paris I began to pay the price of having allowed my need to avoid familiar familial conflict trump doing the right thing. The price I paid was guilt.

A History of Failure

Mike and I had not always had a good relationship. I was four years older, and like most brothers I sometimes took care of him but other times excluded and bullied him.

We lived in a neighborhood that was built during the post-World War II cookie-cutter housing boom. My parents married in early November 1945. In September 1946, I was born. On our block, Mike tried to hang with us older boys, which aggravated me. Because the neighborhood friends usually congregated in my backyard, I would chase Mike indoors. Exclusion was probably natural given our age difference. I was involved in activities in which a younger brother could not participate or compete.

And sometimes I bullied him. There was good-natured big-brother-little-brother bullying. One night he was washing the dishes and I was drying. Every time I turned my back, he flicked dishwater on me. I warned him to stop. As I walked away, water splattered my head. So I opened a bottled Coke, then walked up behind him and turned it upside-down in his pocket.

But not all of my bullying was so good natured. In my senior year of high school, I came home drunk. Mike was awake, and I threatened him with retribution if he squealed to Mama or Dad.

After learning of Mike's suicide, as I walked around Paris wondering what I should have done, many of the bullying episodes, our boyhood arguments, and my self-important exclusion of him came to mind. Of course, I also recalled the good times when we were laughing, joking, and having fun.

But my older-brother way of pushing Mike aside tended to remain in the fore. From a theological standpoint, I could understand the source of my cruelty to a younger brother. Humans are flawed due to the Fall, and our nature leads us to do the things that serve our self-interest. Psychologically, I can identify factors that fueled my cruelty as well. I had an alcoholic father who was cruel when he was drinking and a mother who often was absent from our home due to being hospitalized without warning. Yada-yada. My self-justifications sounded lame even to my rationalizing self.

Of course, I had many memories of good times with Mike. Mama didn't drive and Dad was a railroader, out of town three out of four weeks. Our family went to church infrequently, but I somehow developed a love of church. When I was old enough to walk the two miles there, I started going on my own. And when Mike was old enough to make the walk, I took him with me. Those were good times, brother to brother, talking as we walked to church. We talked about God, school, girls, and sports. I liked to see myself as the wise, advice-giving big brother.

Despite our financially strapped background, Mike grew up a responsible man of God who worked for many years as an IRS auditor. He read books of ali types but loved history the most. And he had a great personality, always ready with a clever comment and spontaneous laugh.

HEAD KNOWLEDGE VERSUS HEART KNOWLEDGE

The flashbacks to some of our family interactions and my interactions with Mike set me into an emotional fog. As Kirby and I strolled through art galleries and around historical sites in Paris, I had lots of time to ruminate. But in those first days after finding out Mike had committed suicide, I didn't so much think as I played in my mental DVD a jumbled mix of scenes. I could not organize my thoughts. Something seemed terribly wrong about losing a younger brother. I had coped with my father's death in 1991, after his yearlong bout with lung cancer, and even Mama's murder in 1996 at age seventy-eight. They both had lived long lives—though never, it seems, long enough. But Mike's death in 2005 was different.

Intellectually, I understood the difference. I also knew that I could not have forced Mike to deal with his posttraumatic stress disorder (PTSD) and that I could not have prevented his suicide. But my intellect wasn't causing the turmoil. My emotions were.

When a younger sibling dies, that off-time death stuns those who are left behind. Suicide adds unbalance to pain. It upsets the fruit stand and sets one scrambling and lurching after fruit bouncing wildly in all directions. And as I chased the scattering images of my brother, I could only hope that I could make some sense out of his death—and soon.

Part 2

Self-Forgiveness 101: A Quick Immersion Course

3

The Tsunami of Self-Blame and Shame

How self-condemnation can destroy your life

> Those of us who have experienced the suicide of a loved one are like survivors of the Titanic. Our lives are irrevocably divided into "before" and "after." It is something we will never forget, a tragedy that will affect us for the rest of our lives.
>
> —Albert Y. Hsu

Life, in many ways, is like making a collage. We take colored paper from this bin, pictures from that bin, and glue from some other bin. At first it seems as if we are slapping the materials on the poster board willy-nilly. Later, however, we use our experiences with composition and perspective to arrange the materials into a meaningful account of a life-altering experience.

Some of the images are stuck fast, and we build meaning around them. Others are malleable. And sometimes, years after the glue dries, we revisit the collage, and—because one part has faded, another part fallen aside—we reexamine the story that is told there. We often find that we need to shift pieces of the collage to make current sense.

Mike's death scrambled my collage. My life didn't make sense as it had three days earlier. I berated myself. I allowed self-condemnation, with its associated self-blame and shame, to worm its way into my life. And I was miserable.

Self-Condemnation Is Everywhere

Life is full of shame and self-blame. Most of the time it remains in the background. But now, as I was caught in a full-blown tsunami of self-blame, I thought back to years of doing psychotherapy and couple therapy. Countless couples had been torn apart by marital conflict and infidelities. Amid the rage, as they described what was tearing them apart, there was shame: the ducked head, averted eyes.

In my work as a clinical scientist who studies forgiveness, I often have encountered the self-blame that seems to run through people's lives. I conducted a group during the making of the documentary movie *The Power of Forgiveness.*[1]

The group was working on forgiving others, but one group member said, "The person I cannot forgive is me. Can I work on that?" Of course he could. And he did, on camera.

An incredible number of movies have taken self-forgiveness as a theme. If movies reflect the problems people struggle with, then, as a culture, we must struggle a lot with self-condemnation. This shouldn't surprise us. Wrongs are committed every day, and every wrong is closely associated with at least one wrongdoer. Some who wrong others are shame-prone and blame themselves. Just think about the plots of movies that weave self-forgiveness into the fabric of the movie. Here are a few: *Beauty and the Beast, The Breakfast Club, Crash, Dead Man Walking, Dreamgirls, It's a Wonderful Life, Regarding Henry, Scrooge, Shrek, Slumdog Millionaire, The Shawshank Redemption,* and *The Sixth Sense.*

We find the same thing with literature. For example, *The Idiot* and *The Brothers Karamazov,* both by Fyodor Dostoyevsky; *A Christmas Carol* by Charles Dickens; *Les Misérables* by Victor Hugo; *A Time to Kill* by John Grisham; *Sophie's Choice* by William Styron; and even *The Grinch Who Stole Christmas* by Dr. Seuss—have self-condemnation at their center.

History, with all its tragedy, is populated by people struggling with shame and self-blame. Corrie ten Boom and her sister Betsie were prisoners in Ravensbrück during World War II—sentenced to the death camp for harboring Jewish refugees in their home in Holland. Betsie always seemed the woman of faith in contrast to Corrie's woman with clay feet. Once they saw a guard mercilessly beating a woman prisoner. "Oh, what a poor creature!" said Corrie. "Yes," said Betsie, "we must pray for him." When Betsie finally died, within months of the war's end, her last words to Corrie were, "We must tell people after the war. There is no pit so deep that God is not deeper still. They will listen to us. We've been there."[2]

Betsie was released to be with her Lord. Corrie went on to tell millions of people through her book (and later movie) *The Hiding Place.*[3] Corrie was chastened by Betsie's faith, but Corrie avoided debilitating shame because she took her failures not to heart, but to God's heart.

As we see from these examples, the stories of personal shame and self-blame are depicted in history, literature, and pop culture. The societal cost of self-condemnation probably runs to the billions of dollars, if you could add up the loss of productivity, creativity, and personal investment in society that is buried in self-condemnation. Self-blame leads to depression, anxiety, and stress disorders. It costs businesses millions of dollars in issues of employee conflict, loss of efficiency, missed time at work, and hiring and retraining new employees when workers quit as a result of having suffered some shaming personal interaction.

I should already have been well aware of this destructive power. But when self-blame and shame flooded my life, I was powerless to escape the damaging embrace. It took years before I was able to break free from the two villains. Now I want to use my expertise and personal experience to help you or someone you know gain the necessary knowledge and skills to struggle victoriously against them.

Self-condemnation can have roots in your past

The movie *Good Will Hunting*[4] tells the story of a young man named Will (Matt Damon) who is more brilliant in mathematics than even the Fields Medal winner, Professor Gerald (Stellan Skarsgård). But Will is personally troubled and in trouble with the law. In a senseless brawl, he violently beats another young man. He is brought before a judge, who considers sentencing Will to a lengthy term of incarceration. But Professor Gerald intervenes by offering Will his freedom if he will agree to psychotherapy and also will commit to study mathematics. Sean (Robin Williams), a college friend of Gerald's, becomes Will's therapist.

Will has a multitude of hang-ups—with a leading problem being that he keeps most people at arm's length. In a pivotal moment, Sean confronts Will after he reveals that a series of foster fathers physically abused him. Sean realizes that Will blames his foster fathers, but he also blames himself for deserving the abuse. Sean tries to get through Will's self-blame. He taps a folder full of photos of Will's bruises, lesions, and burns. He confronts Will's self-blame, "All this stuff, Will? It's not your fault."

Following a heart-wrenching exchange between Will and the therapist, Will begins sobbing. Sean puts his hands on Will's shoulders, and Will grabs him and holds him close, crying. Finally, Will understood the power of self-condemnation to destroy a life. "Unhealthy shame is like a hard shell that we need to crack in order to find the beauty within us," wrote Lewis Smedes.[5] That was certainly true for Will and is true for you and me.

Self-condemnation can begin in childhood

Often self-condemnation originates with experiences in one's family of origin. That was my case. My dad was one of the brightest people I've ever known. Yet he was filled with self-condemnation because he made poor choices at two of life's junctures.

"Are you going to change jobs?" I asked Dad as he was completing his taxes for the year. He had just finished a multiyear accounting course by correspondence.

"No. I'd have to work as a bookkeeper," he said. "I'd make even less than on the railroad. I couldn't support the family. Of course, in a few years I would probably make more money. But we can't afford to live until then." He took a long pull from a can of beer. That might have been the most personal revelation Dad had ever made in my presence.

I wanted to say that if a move was good in the long term, then why not suffer the drop in income for the short term. But I had heard too many lectures about being just a stupid boy. I was not going to open that door and have it slammed in my face.

"I guess I have to decide whether I want to change," my dad said. He upended the beer, then opened the refrigerator door and pulled another can off the shelf. "I don't know. I have responsibilities. I have a family. I'd like to 'aim at the stars'—like somebody said—'because even if you fall short, you're higher than a lamppost.' But with my responsibilities, I have to live with both feet on the ground."

My dad took another long drink. His eyes were drooping a bit. "Yeah, 'aim at the stars,' I always say." He put his head down on the table and remained there, silent. I tiptoed out of the room.

For the rest of his life, my dad regretted that he had passed up important opportunities. He never forgave himself for what he felt was gross inconsistency: being unwilling to take a career risk while holding on to the aim-for-the-stars message, which he often conveyed to me. Self-blame consumed him, and he tried to drown the pain in alcohol.

For me, growing up in this household, self-blame and shame were a big part of the daily fare. A shamed parent can pass his or her shame along to a child. We see, we copy, and we try to avoid similar pitfalls. But shame seems always lying in ambush.

Self-condemnation can be powerful

As a marriage counselor, I had heard versions of this story many times. This one came out in counseling with Marta and Jacob. Marta had gotten involved with Mark, a coworker. They eventually had a one-night affair, and Marta could never relinquish her self-condemnation. In counseling, she said, "Not only was the sex bad, but I was eaten up with guilt. Of course, I told Jacob, and he was very forgiving. In a lot of ways, I wish he had been less so. Because he didn't punish me, I guess I thought I had to punish myself."

Marta told of her downward struggles. Depression consumed her. She couldn't cope, and it affected her work and led to drinking and drug use. "After a year, I was fired. I was a mess. Finally, I wore out Jacob's good graces."

"Where's God in all of this?" I asked.

"Out of the picture," said Marta. "I can't accept that God loves me when I hate myself so much."

Self-condemnation can wreck lives, marriages, families, and careers—as well as a person's relationship with God. Marta was a living example.

Self-condemnation can keep you from going to God

Charlotte Witvliet is an active professor and mother of four (including triplets). She has a sparkling smile and a ready laugh. She is a serious and bright thinker and researcher. At Hope College, she does some of the most labor-intensive studies possible. She measures the body's reactions to transgressions. Her research has found that reliving a past transgression activates sadness, anger, guilt, shame, and muscle tension from a furrowed brow.

Charlotte also studied people who wrote about a wrong they had committed that hurt another person. When they wallowed in their shame, guilt, and the negative impact of the transgression, transgressors felt more self-condemning isolation from God and the victim. Fortunately, other people in the study wrote about repenting for their offense (acknowledging their sorrow about it, and thinking of ways they could apologize, make amends, and change their ways). Repentance reduced self-condemnation and made people want to apologize and right their interpersonal wrongs.

Self-condemnation can be long lasting

John Newton penned the familiar hymn "Amazing Grace." The song has been performed and recorded by musical artists from folk rocker Ani DiFranco to Celtic punk band Dropkick Murphys to the Vienna Boys Choir. (Not to mention my own bouts of singing in the shower.) Everyone knows the song. Not everyone knows the story behind it.

Newton was wealthy. He earned his fortune through the blood and tears of slaves. God's saving power burst onto him, and he left the slave trade. He knew that God could redeem his evil works, that God's mercy was everlasting, and that grace flowed from God's presence. Newton spent the end of his life seeking to undo as much of the harm as possible. He received God's grace, mercy, compassion, and forgiveness, despite his remorse over his early slave trading.[6]

Self-condemnation can motivate people to do good

Self-condemnation isn't all bad. Just as it can damage relationships and drive us further from God, it also can motivate us to do good. We see this theme in popular fiction. One of the neoclassic fables in cinema is *Pretty Woman.*[7] Julia Roberts plays a neophyte hooker named Vivian. Richard Gere portrays Edward, a business shark. He buys struggling businesses, dismantles them, and sells them off piecemeal. Both Vivian and Edward are being slowly consumed by self-condemnation, even though they do not acknowledge it at the time. That feeling does not suck them into the drain. Rather, each treats the other as a person of value. The self-condemnation, guided by redeeming love, transforms them and brings about their redemption by the fable's end.

FREEDOM FROM SELF-CONDEMNATION

This book is about how you, or someone you know, might deal with self-blame and shame. If it is you who is struggling, I hope you'll find yourself in these pages. You might condemn yourself because you've made bad decisions about marriage—perhaps you made a bad choice of a marriage partner, you had an affair, or you lost your marriage through divorce. You might have chosen to live with someone without the commitment of marriage, and now you look back in regret. You might feel that you have shattered your own children by making poor parenting choices. Perhaps you made work decisions on which you now look back and cringe. Maybe you hurt people or treated friends shabbily. The things we do that we later regret are legion.

There also are many things you might wish you had done but failed to act on. At the end of their lives, most people look back and regret the things they didn't do more than the things they did. Are there dreams you didn't chase, goals you didn't reach? Are there tasks you left undone and now wish you could be handed a "do-over"?

What is common about these regrets is not the situation that gives rise to them. That is almost incidental. What *is* common are the responses. Regret. Remorse. Sorrow. Sadness. Grief over lost opportunities. Disappointment. Anger. Disillusionment with ourselves and others. And all too often, we feel disappointment and anger at God that we dare not express. So rather than hash things out with God, we simply try to ignore God, put God on the shelf, or go about life without referring to God or praying. We might become involved in a struggle with God, one that perhaps we cannot admit even to ourselves, much less to others.

All of these experiences are part of self-blame. If you have experienced or are experiencing self-blame, you can emerge from the other end with more resolution and perhaps with self-forgiveness. You can have an understanding that will equip you to defeat self-condemnation and free yourself from the lure of starting down that road again.

Freedom from self-condemnation is like Peter's freedom from jail

Self-blame and shame can imprison you. Peter, no stranger to self-blame due to his threefold denial of Jesus, was ministered to directly by Jesus. After he became an apostle, he spent time in jail until God freed him. That experience can be a metaphor that describes people's release from the captivity of self-condemnation.

In Acts 4:1, 3, the priests, a captain of the temple guard, and the Sadducees imprisoned Peter and John for performing a miracle. In Acts 5:17–18, the high priest and the Sadducees again arrested the apostles. During the night an angel opened the doors and freed them. The next morning, the captain and his officers found the apostles teaching in the temple courts, while the jail remained locked and the guards tended an empty cell (see verse 23).

King Herod got into the act. He had James, John's brother, executed. He arrested Peter, and he was serious about keeping him imprisoned (see Acts 12:1–4). Rather than being returned to a local jail, Peter was taken to a much more secure facility (see Acts 4:3; 5:23). "After arresting him, he put him in prison, handing him over to be guarded by four squads of four soldiers each. Herod intended to bring him out for public trial after the Passover" (Acts 12:4).

We find that Peter was not just thrown into a cell. "Peter was sleeping between two soldiers, bound with two chains, and sentries stood guard at the entrance" (Acts 12:6). But even then, Peter was freed from prison.

An angel appeared and (you gotta love this) "struck Peter on the side and woke him up. 'Quick, get up!' he said, and the chains fell off Peter's wrists" (Acts 12:7). The angel did not disturb the two guards, who were right there, sleeping beside Peter. The angel marched Peter past two sentries at the entrance to the cell. Under the protection of the angel, Peter wound through the prison, passing beneath the noses of additional guards (four squads of four) and other prisoners. "Peter followed him out of the prison.… They passed the first and second guards and came to the iron gate leading to the city. It opened for them by itself, and they went through it. When they had walked the length of one street, suddenly the angel left him" (Acts 12:9–10).

You'll recall how Peter knocked on the door of the house of Mary the mother of John. A servant named Rhoda answered the door and recognized him, but she was so excited that she ran to tell the others, leaving Peter standing in the cold. Those inside had been praying for Peter's release. But when he arrived at the house, they couldn't believe it could really happen.

Moving forward over the barriers that block your freedom

Perhaps you feel imprisoned by self-blame. This image is an apt metaphor for the captivity we experience at the hands of self-blame. Breaking free from self-condemnation requires first that you become aware of the problem—and once you're aware of it, decide to deal with it. Step 1, right at the outset, is to go to God. This is the only way you can escape the confinement of self-blame.

You have been blaming yourself for things you did or said. And in many cases the words or behavior that gave rise to self-blame did, in fact, hurt someone. So whenever possible, go to the people you hurt and make amends. Restore the relationships. You might be saying right now, "I would do that, gladly, if only I knew how." *Moving Forward* provides you with the skills to do so. Step 2 is to repair relationships, which is covered in chapters 9, 10, and 11. Closely aligned with the previous step is the need to deal with negative and unrealistic expectations and to Rethink Ruminations (Step 3). Fight against the mind-set that leads to loss of hope and the assumption that what you did in the past is not redeemable. The truth is this: you are not a "lifer," a prisoner who will never be free.

Moving Forward will walk you through facing the issues squarely, turning to God for help, and determining to do what is necessary to solve the issues that led to your self-blame. And then you will take a step that might be more difficult than all the others added together: make a decision to forgive yourself. Thousands of people have used the REACH emotional self-forgiveness method to move from an emotionally imprisoned state to the freedom that we all seek, but until now have not known how to achieve it.

The REACH Self-Forgiveness method is adapted to apply to your own wrongdoing (Step 4) based on the REACH Forgiveness approach that is summarized in chapter 2. They are the same steps I followed to forgive my mother's murderer, only applied now to forgiving yourself. We will inevitably do and say things that damage others. And unless you are a sociopath, you will inevitably regret those things later on. You also will probably condemn yourself for not having been perfect. You let someone down, you caused hurt or injury.

The truth is, you are human. You have to accept yourself as one who is at the same time flawed, yet precious. This part of the process is all about accepting yourself (Step 5). If you can do that—and it's tough to accept flaws in yourself that might catch you completely off guard—then it is time to face down a hostile parole board that wants to keep you locked up in a self-condemning cell. If you can break free, and that is where we are headed, then you can try to live virtuously from that point onward (Step 6).

Working through the steps touched on above will open the way for you to walk out of the prison of self-blame so you can live a life of virtue based on self-acceptance as a flawed but precious person. The main lesson of this book is that you *can* break free. You can escape the prison of self-blame and shame by following the Six Steps to Self-Forgiveness. Identifying the issues involved and committing yourself to work at achieving a solution will not translate into instant self-forgiveness. Lewis Smedes said about forgiving others, "Forgiving is a journey; the deeper the wound, the longer the journey."[8] Forgiving yourself is no less arduous a journey. However, the outcome is freedom, and who wouldn't prefer that to being locked into a pattern of self-blame for the rest of your life?

4

First Steps Up the Mountain

Peering through the fog, I felt God's presence

> Experience is a hard teacher because she gives the test first and the lesson afterwards.
>
> —Vernon Law

Before you set out, take a close look at what lies ahead. Others have moved forward when they were bogged down in self-condemnation. You can too.

You *Can* Break Free from Self-Condemnation

When I reached the point of starting to do what was necessary to forgive myself, I blundered into it, and my self-blame almost overwhelmed me. I was a Christian, a clinical psychologist, a researcher who studied forgiveness, and most importantly, a normal person who had dealt with friends, family members, and community members as they struggled with their own issues. I had seen lots of self-blame and shame—but always from the outside. It felt different going through it myself, when my life was being torn in two by shame. But I finally was able to apply the steps and came out of it intact. I now can relate what I learned, not as an impartial observer, but as a full participant. I did it. So can you.

In the following chapters we will look at the stories of people who struggled with self-blame and see how they got past their struggles. I hope that my story and the stories of others will convey principles and practices that will help you. They did it. So can you.

Viktor E. Frankl overcame the past. Frankl was a psychiatrist in Austria in the years leading up to World War II. Like millions of other Europeans, he was removed from his city and held as a prisoner at several Nazi death camps. He understood suffering. "It's like a gas," he wrote, "that fills up a whole room once it's squirted in." But suffering is not the end game. "We who lived in the concentration camps can remember the men who walked through the huts comforting others, giving away their last piece of bread. They may have been few in number, but they offer sufficient proof that everything can be taken from a man but one thing: the last of the human freedoms—to choose one's attitude in a given set of circumstances, to choose one's own way."[1]

But we do not want to try doing it on our own. Self-condemnation can be like a plant with prickly thorns. Its roots snake underground in a complex web and rise near the surface to thrust new sticker-bushes into the path of anyone who might come along. But—and here's the good news—it also is an invitation to come to Jesus. Too often we focus on the guilt of our wrongdoing and sense that it separates us from God. Yes, guilt *should* make us feel separated from God. And this spiritual estrangement should make us miserable. But God did not design us to stay separate and miserable, nor to try to fix our own guilt. I can't repair it, and neither can you. Both of us should realize that by now.

Jesus welcomes sinners. So we can come to Jesus for his healing, his forgiveness, his freedom, and his cleansing and renewing. Instead of letting ourselves be tormented by guilt, we can take it to Jesus. That is how the good news works. Conviction for our sin is not intended to torture us with guilt and shame. Jesus wants us to bring our sin to him so that we can be cleansed.

Self-condemnation can thus be an impetus to humility. We cannot defeat self-condemnation alone. Trying to do so is a natural response to pain and suffering, but it doesn't work. What does work is to do what never comes naturally to us, and that is to rely on God.

Because of this, self-condemnation can trigger virtue. It can be an opportunity to receive comfort from God and to seek out those we have wronged to attempt to make things right. God offers us freedom from bondage. As Romans 8:31 tells us, God is for us; who can be against us? However, when we continue to condemn ourselves, we agree to remain in bondage. When we embrace self-blame rather than coming to God for help, we are denying God's desire to set us free (see Isaiah 61:1; Luke 4:18). If we draw close, God will set us free, forgiving and freeing us to forgive ourselves. If you are struggling to break out of self-blame and shame, choose love, not power, as your way out. Then self-forgiveness will come—as will many other benefits.

MY THREE DAYS IN THE TOMB

I had this knowledge of self-blame and shame, but for three days after Mike's suicide it did me no good. I walked around Paris in an emotional fog. I felt sadness, grief, regret, disappointment, anger, worry, and even curiosity and dread. Those emotions swirled around in me. I couldn't disentangle them.

I felt the usual experiences that people have when they lose someone close to them. I felt the sense of being unmoored, cut loose from the stable dock of my identity as Mike's brother. I wanted to undo the past. I would say things like, "If only I had encouraged Mike more to seek counseling"; "If only I had been available for him to call"; "If only I had not bullied him when we were kids, maybe he wouldn't have rejected my suggestion about seeking counseling." This type of self-criticism is common when a person is grieving. But simply knowing that to be true didn't make it easier to cope with.

I also dealt with anger and depression caused by the knowledge that we could never recapture our relationship. I was angry at Mike for taking his life and abandoning his wife and child (and *me,* his brother). I also was tormented with curiosity and dread over what Mike's suicide note said. Why would he address the note to me and not to his wife? Feelings, thoughts, and concerns swirled and bubbled like foam in a boiling cauldron.

My brother's death introduced me to a deep internal struggle far beyond anything I had dealt with before. In the past I'd had regrets. Everyone does. But most of the things I might blame myself for melted away under the heat of critical reflection and confession to God. I had never struggled with unremitting, obsessive regret like I was now facing.

The guilt I felt was not wholly undeserved. But the guilt was mixed with a self-pitying sorrow. I had lost someone who was important to me, and now I could never do anything to redeem my mistakes. *Now I am left to slow cook in memories of my meanness,* I thought, self-absorbed. I confessed my sins to God. But I also poked and prodded myself to prolong the self-torture.

As Kirby and I mined European art in Paris museums, I excavated my past. Feelings welled up and subsided. I could hardly lift my feet to walk. A stench, like rotten vegetation, sometimes seemed to waft across me. Sometimes the quicksand of emotions would pull me under.

A sudden memory

Walking across the square in front of Notre Dame Cathedral, I stopped suddenly. "I just remembered that Mike and I went to vacation Bible school one summer at Fort Hill Baptist Church."

"Did something happen there?" Kirby asked.

"Near the end of the week we were in a big assembly." Sharp images flooded my mind. "The pastor gave a stirring talk. I was motivated to make a commitment to Jesus. But I fought it. Then I saw Mike rise from the seat next to me to make a public profession of his belief."

"You must have been happy for him."

"I wish. But my feelings were darker. I was embarrassed that I had not gone forward and my little brother had. I was angry. I felt that he had shown me up."

"You felt competitive."

"Not often. But he was so much younger than I was, and, well, I had wanted to act but couldn't bring myself to do it. Then, to make things worse, as we walked home, I berated him for falling for the emotional appeal."

"You must have felt horrible," she said.

"Even then I felt I had somehow desecrated something that was pure," I said. "But that didn't stop me from trying to ruin his experience."

"I'm sure that God has forgiven you." Kirby threw me lifelines to drag me dripping from the bog, but I was so wrapped up in my feelings that it was difficult to accept her love and support. I started walking again, head down.

Fog and an open door

On the third day, I awakened before six o'clock. The light was faint. I couldn't get back to sleep, and I had already settled into my morose brooding. I realized I needed to try to kick myself out of this.

"I'm going for a run," I told Kirby. "Can you wait breakfast till I get back?"

"I'll try to sleep a little more," she said.

As I stepped outside, cool morning mist slapped me alert. I began to jog. Bread shops sprayed tempting smells into the north Paris streets. My skin tingled as cool mist condensed on it. I settled into a slow pace. My feet slapped the damp pavement. After twenty minutes of winding through the streets, I found myself at the foot of Montmartre, the little mountain near the hotel where we were staying. I saw the steps winding upward into the hazy cool of the morning.

Kirby and I had been up there a couple of times earlier in the week. We could look out over the city, then descend and picnic on the grass. At the top sat La Basilique du Sacré Coeur. From the balcony of the area in front of the cathedral was my favorite view of Paris. From there, I knew I could see the beauty of the city stretching out before me.

I needed to run up the stairs to the top of Montmartre and take in that view. I trudged up the steps, puffing until I reached the top. I wandered over to the little wall that marks a perfect observation point from which to enjoy the city. The view was obscured by fog so that I could barely make out that there was a city below. But here and there, domes from churches poked heavenward through a cotton-wool blanket of fog.

I thought, *This is a picture of the way I've been feeling all week since hearing of Mike's death. I am in an emotional fog.*

I turned to look at the cathedral. To my surprise, the doors were open—unusual for 6:30 a.m. Inside, cleaners were vacuuming. I looked down the aisle of the grand sanctuary to a large painting of Jesus. His arms were outstretched; his heart was pouring out blood and water. As I looked at that magnificent picture, I thought, *I am not the only person to experience loss, grief, and disappointment. I am not the only person to have ever felt the pain and anguish of losing someone. Jesus, at death, gave up his relationship with his Father on our behalf. And what's better, Jesus, now resurrected, is here going through my suffering with me.*

The fog that had been swirling around me for the last three days lifted. I felt at peace. I thought, *Jesus might not always pull us out of the fiery furnace, but at least he walks with us through the fire.* I knew in my heart, not in my mind, that in this struggle I was not alone. With Jesus's help I would try to forgive myself. I'd tackle it, I thought, just as soon as we could get settled at the University of Cambridge.

A Brief Retreat

In August 2005, though, before taking the new position in England, Kirby and I dashed back to the United States for a week. I had to give a talk at the Chautauqua Institution in upstate New York. The institution invites speakers to teach on their specialties. The people live in an open and friendly community of intellectually engaged people dealing with exciting ideas.

Steven Post, director of the Institute for Research on Unlimited Love (IRUL), organized a symposium on altruistic, unlimited love. Steven saw forgiveness as part of unlimited love, and he invited me to give one of the talks. It was just six weeks after Mike's suicide.

"I'm kind of nervous about this talk," I confided to Kirby as we flew back to the United States. "I will talk mostly about forgiveness, as Steven has asked me, but I will probably mention my struggles with self-blame. I might get into self-forgiveness, but I don't have much to say about it."

"I thought you advised one of your graduate students on her thesis about self-forgiveness," Kirby said.

"Yes, but she found that, while most people do move more toward self-forgiveness over time, the picture her data give is not clear."

"I know you'll have something to say," she said, always more confident in me than I am in myself.

During my talk at Chautauqua, I mentioned Mike's suicide. I admitted openly that I had not been able to forgive myself for many of my failures as a brother and even for my failures as a clinical psychologist. I said that I had no answers—only many questions. I closed by saying, "I hope that someday I will be able to forgive myself. Then maybe I'll be able to bring what I learn to help other people forgive themselves so they can live healthier and happier lives."

Later, an elderly woman was sitting next to me at another talk. "Do you think self-forgiveness is good for a person's health?" she asked. "I was at your talk yesterday, and you ended the talk saying that you thought that self-forgiveness was good for people's health."

"We haven't studied that question directly," I said. "But we know that holding a grudge or holding vengeful attitudes toward someone who has harmed or offended you can keep your stress reactions turned on—especially if the grudge lasts a long time. I think holding a grudge against ourselves is, if anything, worse."

"Why worse?"

"Well, with someone else who has hurt or offended us, we can at least escape the person. But we can't get away from ourselves. So if we are blaming ourselves for something, or if we are blaming ourselves because we can't live up to our standards or the standards of someone else, or if we can't accept ourselves as imperfect people, then we live with that self-blame longer and more intimately than we might live with a grudge against someone else."

After a week at Chautauqua, Kirby and I made our way to Cambridge. It was at Cambridge, at the Institute for Psychology and Christianity, that I got my first real glimpse of understanding self-forgiveness.

5

The Life-Changing Benefits of Self-Forgiveness

Taking an unsparing look at your life is never easy

> We are supposed to forgive everyone; everyone includes ourselves.
>
> —Denis Waitley

Before you embark on the Six Steps to Self-Forgiveness, it's important to consider why following these steps is important. Not everyone struggling with self-condemnation will want to break free merely because they will feel better or because self-condemnation stands between them and a closer relationship with God. So let's look at a few of the many ways the freedom of self-forgiveness will open you up to positive events and experiences.

SELF-FORGIVENESS WILL FREE YOU FROM...

Guilt. Guilt will weigh you down, and feelings of guilt are not always deserved. Sometimes guilt arises over unrealistic expectations and standards of perfection that none of us can achieve. When you are able to forgive yourself, that weight is lifted.

Self-blame. Self-forgiveness frees you from the chattering, accusing voice in your head. The constant voice of blame—coming from Satan, temptations, or self-accusation—slows or stops completely when you forgive yourself.

Stress-related illness. Self-forgiveness can improve your health,[1] and here's why. Holding on to self-condemnation elevates your stress, which has been associated with a long list of physical and psychological harm. Chronic stressfulness can elevate cortisol, as we have shown by looking at people in failed versus happy marriages. Cortisol is a neurohormone that is secreted to break fatty materials down into easy-to-access blood sugar or glucose—which is helpful in responding to danger.

Chronic stress, however, creates elevated levels of cortisol, which can be harmful in the long run if it remains at an unnecessarily high level. High chronic cortisol[2] can (1) shrink the size of the cortex (I personally do not have enough spare cortex that I want mine diminished); (2) make people depressed, anxious, or angry; (3) cause dysfunction of the immune system; (4) affect sexual desire and ability to conceive; and (5) put us at risk for colitis, ulcers, and elimination problems. Probably the most severe effect that cortisol has, though, is on the cardiovascular system. Cortisol can elevate your risk of having a heart attack, stroke, and other dangerous cardiovascular events. But by learning to forgive yourself, you can lower chronic stressfulness.

Alcohol misuse. My friend Jon Webb is a burly teddy bear of a guy. He is friendly, he cares for his students, and he is dogged in his study of the relationship between lack of forgiveness and problems associated with alcohol misuse. I met Jon at the international forgiveness conference in 2003. He and his colleagues at East Tennessee State University conducted a longitudinal study on substance abuse and religion. [3] They assessed forgiveness of self, of others, and from God at both an initial baseline and at a six-month follow-up. People who abused alcohol reported that their success in forgiving themselves lagged behind the forgiveness of others or forgiveness from God. Higher forgiveness of self at baseline was related to fewer drinking consequences at follow-up six months later. Higher forgiveness of self and of others was associated with less use of alcohol at both time points. Webb and his colleagues concluded that, overall, forgiveness of the self might be, for alcoholics, the most difficult type of forgiveness to achieve. But if they were able to do so, it could help control their drinking.

Accusation. Satan loves to accuse us (see Job 1:9–11; 2:4–5). Scripture calls Satan the accuser (see Revelation 12:10), and we all know his accusations can be oppressive. We know from Scripture that we are to resist his accusations (see James 4:7). By bringing our sins to God and receiving God's forgiveness, we can then forgive ourselves and we can rest in the knowledge that the accusations of Satan are groundless. If we forgive ourselves, we can silence the oppressive voice of the enemy.

Self-absorption. Self-forgiveness can also free you from an unhealthy focus on your own concerns. If I condemn myself, I become absorbed in myself and my flaws. By being able to forgive myself, I can avoid this snare.

SELF-FORGIVENESS PROVIDES FREEDOM FOR...

Flourishing. Forgiving yourself does not end with freeing you from negative experiences. It also frees you to flourish. By not being so wrapped up in self-condemnation, you can enjoy more pleasurable and positive experiences. And you can act more virtuously—which will help you feel better about your life as you find even more ways to bless others.

Focusing on God. Instead of being wrapped up in condemning yourself for past failures, you can seek God and enjoy that relationship. When people condemn themselves, they often incorrectly think God is displeased with them. But think about Jesus's response to a woman caught in adultery: "Then neither do I condemn you.… Go now and leave your life of sin." (John 8:11). God is more interested in restorative justice than in punitive justice.

Focusing on others. Self-forgiveness allows you to focus on others, with the goal of helping to meet their needs. This is what all of us are supposed to do, according to Jesus's commandments to love God above all things and to love our neighbor the same way we love ourselves (see Mark 12:29–31). In addition, forgiving others can release oxytocin, the bonding peptide that can forge a link between people.[4] It is very speculative, but forgiving ourselves might free us to attend to others instead of focusing on our own pain, and that would allow more oxytocin to be produced, resulting in better relationships all around. It also is possible that self-forgiveness releases oxytocin, perhaps enhancing greater self-esteem.

Health. Self-forgiveness frees you to experience better health.[5] The absence of illness is not the same as the presence of good health. Self-forgiveness provides energy and vitality. It supplies both a freedom from the past and a forward-thinking orientation that helps you seek the benefits of exercise, a healthy diet, and energetic work. It's like Spider Man swinging through the urban jungle. He shoots out a web and swings on it, but at the end of that trajectory, he has to turn loose of the old web and shoot a new web forward. Self-forgiveness cuts your ties to old worry and propels you forward on a more healthful trajectory.

Self-forgiveness aids good health in two ways: by inhibiting illness and by fueling the habits of good health. Positive psychology researcher Barbara Fredrickson has identified numerous positive effects that occur when negative emotions are replaced by positive ones.[6] Our outlook is broadened—making us more open to new positive experiences that can promote health. Also, forgiveness builds our resources for dealing with difficulties and for pursuing our goals and dreams. Thus, our energy, vitality, and positive motivation are increased when we feel less negative and more positive about ourselves.

And just as positive emotions generate multiple benefits in your life and health, so does self-forgiveness. Ann Macaskill and her colleagues surveyed 324 British undergraduates. Those who rated themselves as higher in self-forgiveness also rated their general health better.[7]

Better quality of life. Catherine Romero and her colleagues studied eighty-one women during the time they were being treated for breast cancer.[8] Both a self-forgiving attitude and spirituality were related to less mood disturbance and better quality of life. A year later, a team conducting nearly identical research found that women who blamed themselves for their breast cancer reported more mood disturbance and poorer quality of life. In contrast, those who did not blame themselves reported less mood disturbance and less of an impact on their quality of life. Self-forgiveness doesn't cure cancer, as I and colleagues found from reviewing several studies. But once a person has been diagnosed with cancer, as with the women Romero studied, self-forgiveness can matter greatly in enhancing one's quality of life.

Peace. Self-forgiveness, finally, will help you experience peace. People who continue to wrestle with self-blame are unsettled. They find it difficult to exhale and relax. Forgiving yourself will help you live at peace.

When we look rationally at self-blame versus self-forgiveness, with all that it provides freedom from and for, we can shake our heads in wonder that we would ever hold on to self-blame and fight off self-forgiveness. Yet often that seems exactly what we do. Let's look at what makes forgiving ourselves so difficult.

6

Why It Is So Difficult to Forgive Yourself

You know yourself better than anyone else—and that's part of the struggle

> We must develop and maintain the capacity to forgive. He who is devoid of the power to forgive is devoid of the power to love.… There is some good in the worst of us and some evil in the best of us. When we discover this, we are less prone to hate our enemies.
>
> —Martin Luther King Jr.

Self-blame is often inextricably tied up with shame, and shame adds to your stress level. An inability to let go of shame and self-blame can feed anger, anxiety, depression, and low self-esteem.

People who are caught in self-blame and shame try to cope with their stress. Sometimes they succeed; sometimes they don't. Humans are remarkably creative in trying out ways to cope, and what works for one person does not necessarily work for another. Some people simply blame others. Others give in to suffering and take on the mantle of victim. Some simply try to make excuses for their past failings, as a way to wriggle off the hook. Or they resort to denial, assuming they have done nothing wrong and trying hard not to look too closely at their past. Usually, however, that strategy doesn't work.

While the ineffective strategies might give you a sense of working hard to overcome your shame, it is far better to learn the one practice that has been shown—in research and in the lives of many thousands of people—to be effective over the long term. I am referring, of course, to responsible self-forgiveness and self-acceptance.

TWO TYPES OF SELF-FORGIVENESS

There are two types of self-forgiveness. One is to make a decision about how you intend to act toward yourself. I call that *decisional self-forgiveness.* When you decide to forgive, you make a statement of intention to treat yourself as a valuable person. That means, in part, that you will no longer seek retaliation against yourself. In other words, you will no longer feel the need to punish yourself for past failings.

Instead, you decide to value yourself. You might still, at times, feel guilty and even angry with yourself. But you decide that you will not allow negative emotions to dominate your behavior. Instead, you will treat yourself with the respect that all humans deserve. As Corrie ten Boom said, "Forgiveness is an act of the will, and the will can function regardless of the temperature of the heart."[1]

The second type of self-forgiveness is *emotional self-forgiveness,* which involves replacing negative, unforgiving emotions with positive emotions toward yourself. It is emotional self-forgiveness that cools the heat of anger in your heart; it's what Corrie ten Boom referred to as "the temperature of the heart." The emotions that we use to replace negative, unforgiving emotions are empathy, sympathy, compassion, and love for ourselves.

Later in the book we will look in detail at the steps involved in replacing negative emotions with positive. But first, it's helpful to understand why doing this is so difficult for all of us.

WHY SELF-FORGIVENESS IS SO DIFFICULT

"In the last part of my talk today, I'm going to discuss self-forgiveness," I told an audience of about one hundred people who came to hear about forgiveness—God's forgiveness, forgiveness of ourselves, and forgiveness of others. A woman in the third row showed sudden interest. Her hand shot up. "Is it harder to forgive yourself or someone else?" Clearly, she had not posed a strictly academic question. Fear edged the intensity in her voice.

I answered, "It often depends on the size of the transgression. It certainly is easier to forgive yourself for a minor oversight than to forgive a jerk boyfriend for cheating on you. But, for the same degree of harm, I think often it is harder to forgive yourself. There have been some studies of this." Here are some of the things I described.

Studies show that forgiving yourself is different from forgiving others

The Psychological Studies Institute, [2] a Christian counseling training program located just north of Atlanta, pioneered the study of traits of forgiveness of oneself and others. Paul Mauger and his colleagues studied outpatient clients in psychotherapy and found that forgiveness of self and forgiveness of others were only modestly related to each other.[3] This finding has been confirmed in numerous other studies.[4] But the next discovery by Mauger and his colleagues cinched it. Each type of forgiveness was found to relate to different scale scores on personality measures.

Again, this finding has been replicated frequently in separate research.[5] Chronic self-condemnation was related to higher client anxiety, depression, and negative self-esteem. Those with trouble forgiving others were more angry and hostile.

Still, perhaps people who had problems that bothered them enough to seek psychotherapy might be different from people who were not having such severe emotional problems. Ann Macaskill and her colleagues in England showed, for example, that low forgiveness of self in British college undergraduates was related to high tendencies to react emotionally to transgressions.[6] Scott Ross and his coauthors found the same thing with students in the United States.[7] Macaskill also found that women were more prone to self-condemnation than were men.[8]

Self-forgiveness and forgiveness of others are different, and the people who struggle the most with each type of forgiveness differ. The struggles themselves differ, and the intensity of the experience can differ. But why?

Possible explanations

Mental gymnastics are required. When you attempt to forgive someone else for an offense, you are adopting the viewpoint of the forgiver. The wrongdoer, of course, is someone other than yourself. However, when you try to forgive yourself, you have to operate from two points of view—*both* forgiver and wrongdoer. Holding contrasting points of view at the same time is a strain. It is hard to bounce back and forth from one perspective to the other.

No escape. Forgiving the self is also difficult because we are stuck with our thoughts 24/7. We cannot get away from ourselves.

Insider information. Part of the difficulty in forgiving yourself is because you have insider information about who you really are, what your deepest motivations are, when you have a hidden agenda or ulterior motive, when you are being forthright, and when you are deliberately obscuring the facts. We try to assume the best about ourselves, but it's impossible to maintain this position. In our quieter moments, we are confronted with the unflattering truth. The fact is, we know too much about ourselves. We know that we are capable of repeating the same wrong even when we know how hurtful it is. We also know that, as much as we profess love for God, we are like Paul who wrote: "I do not understand what I do. For what I want to do I do not do, but what I hate I do" (Romans 7:15). That is, we know the weakness of our will to do the right thing. Our transgression—of which we are so ashamed—is often an indication of a pattern. *We dare not simply let ourselves off the hook for this,* we think, *because we will turn around and do exactly the same thing tomorrow.* Or maybe something worse.

We wrong others. We do not merely hurt ourselves when we do wrong. We usually have wronged someone else. We know that God does not approve of wrongdoing. Therefore, we know that, regardless of what we did to another person, we have sinned more seriously against God. So forgiving ourselves is not simply a matter of letting ourselves off the hook. Imagine how you would react if Hitler had been tried at Nuremberg and, on the witness stand, had defended his evil actions: "I admit that I did a lot of bad things, killed a lot of innocent people. But I have decided to forgive myself." Virtually all of us would say, "No way. You can't just let yourself off the hook. You have to deal with God and try to repair some of the harm you caused."

Most of us realize that we have an obligation to try to repair some of the social damage that we have done, even if we have already confessed those sins to God. But even when we go to the persons we wronged to seek their forgiveness and reconciliation, it's still tough to forgive ourselves. We try to take care of it with the magic words "I forgive myself." But we can't simply say the words and then experience complete freedom.

Thus, we add to our load of self-blame when we fail to forgive ourselves, and it multiplies our shame and sense of failure.

The wrongdoer must pay. You might find it more difficult to forgive yourself because it's common to feel that the burden of repairing wrongdoing is on the person who committed the act. But when you are looking at your own wrongdoing, *you* are the guilty party. Your sense of justice seems to require some degree of self-punishment. At the same time, facing up to the fact of being the wrongdoer damages your sense of self.

Add all this up, and it's easy to see why forgiving ourselves is so hard. Let's take a look at what self-forgiveness and self-acceptance have to do within the organization of our Self.

THE SELF SYSTEM

When we condemn ourselves for doing wrong or failing to live up to our standards, it attacks our self-esteem. Psychologists tell us that we have a three-part Self system.[9] The Self is composed of (1) the true self (the way we really are as God sees us); (2) a concept of ourselves that we *think* is real (our concept of our real self); and (3) a concept of the way we think we ought to be (our ideal self).[10] In comparing the three concepts of self, we develop high self-esteem if our real self-concept comes close to matching our ideal self.

How the parts work

It is possible to acknowledge the inconsistencies between the three parts of the Self system yet still not accept yourself. For most of us, the inability to accept ourselves is more debilitating than an inability to forgive ourselves. Whenever we sense—through conscious thought or through beyond-the-conscious-mind awareness—that the parts of our Self system are inconsistent, we feel anxious. With that anxiety comes a threat to the Self, and we try to defend against it.

Struggles with self-acceptance usually occur because our concept of our real self does not match up well with our ideal self. This might be because we are ashamed of things we did in the past. We can't understand or accept how we could have done something like that. Or we have done wrong within the range of typical human behavior, yet hold unrealistic ideals that are satisfied with nothing less than our own perfection. The conceptual inconsistencies often spring from the contrast between the true self, which God recognizes to be flawed, and our concept of the real self, which resists the idea of our flawed being. Or the anxiety might arise from maintaining an image of our ideal self defined by standards that are impossibly high or unreasonably low.

When we detect inconsistencies between the real self (as we see ourselves) and the true self (God's view of us), we usually defend ourselves unconsciously and move on. But when we perceive gaping inconsistencies, or when rumination continues to bring the inconsistencies into our awareness, self-blame and shame will almost always follow. Rumination is obsessively dwelling on negative thoughts and images. It is like playing familiar, old (yet hated) class-B movies over and over in your mind. When you ruminate, you keep returning to the worst parts of your life.

Standards and expectations are lodged in the ideal self and originate from our families and cultural expectations. Our concept of the ideal self also can be influenced by our beliefs about what God wants of us, how we think God perceives us, and how we see God. If we see God as a harsh, judgmental, and punitive Authority, we will likely be motivated to avoid negative consequences. That inhibits our creative pursuit of positive actions. We might see ourselves somewhere between the extremes of a hardworking striver to achieve God's favor (that we fear will never be experienced) and a beaten and cynical skeptic that says he or she has no need of God's approval. In contrast, if we see God as a permissive, completely accepting grandparent who wouldn't want to see us hurt, we will likely see ourselves ideally somewhere between an irresponsible, self-centered person looking out for number one and someone secure in love but with little motivation to achieve.

Christian theologies differ on the view of whether it is possible for a Christian to achieve moral perfection on earth. However, most theologies agree that while humans are fallen and exhibit the effects of that on a daily basis, at the same time they are of immeasurable value to God. Lewis Smedes put it like this:

> The amazing grace that saved a wretch like me brings with it the discovery that I am worthy of the grace that saves. I know that wretches like me do not deserve amazing grace; it would hardly be amazing grace if we had it coming. But we can be worthy of it even though we do not deserve it. This is what grace can reveal.[11]

At first we recoil from what Smedes says, but for everyone who has ever held a baby in their arms, we can come to understand it. The just-born infant has done nothing to deserve our love. Yet the baby is worth loving.

Imagine that I own a painting by impressionist Pierre-Auguste Renoir. It is worth millions of dollars. It isn't perfect, but it is still worth millions. What if I did not treat it as a valuable work of art? Suppose I hung it in my basement and never went down there to enjoy its beauty. It is still worth millions, regardless of how it is treated. Suppose I deface it, and later an expert restores the painting to its former glory. It is still worth millions.

This is the way most Christian theologies view the ideal self. Yet for individual Christians or people who have been influenced by a negative

Christian culture, it is hard to get past the ugly scars we have suffered. It is difficult for most of us to accept that there is something of real and precious worth beneath the flawed surface.

Christian theology also professes that God knows people's hearts and the Holy Spirit can convict people of wrongdoing (see John 16:8). Also, God is willing to search and try our hearts (see Psalm 139:23–24) if we ask. God reveals our heart as we pray, read Scripture, seek wise counsel from other Christians, live in community with other people of faith, seek discernment, and look at what can be learned through the circumstances of life.

Self-acceptance is a necessary step in reconciling the true self, the real self, and the ideal self. It is the only way you can live at peace with yourself.

WHAT IS REQUIRED FOR SELF-FORGIVENESS

The recent, leading work on self-forgiveness was begun in 2005 by Judith Hall and Frank Fincham.[12] Fincham is one of the most prolific researchers in the field of psychology. His specialty is couple relationships. Hall was a graduate student who learned research with Fincham, and now she is a post-PhD psychological scientist.

Hall and Fincham recognized that few psychologists had studied self-forgiveness, even though some people, including the pioneer in studying forgiveness, Robert Enright, had written about it earlier.[13]

In 2005 Hall and Fincham defined self-forgiveness as changing one's motivation so that one is less likely to be harsh and hurtful to the self and more likely to be kind and compassionate toward the self. They said self-forgiveness was different from what they called pseudo self-forgiveness, letting oneself off the hook without accepting responsibility for one's acts.

They suggested that self-forgiveness was harder if a person has a higher sense of guilt. One's own offenses are harder to forgive if guilt is a nagging voice of conscience. Self-forgiveness also is more difficult, they have argued, if one thinks negatively toward oneself, which leads to shame and inhibits self-forgiveness. Self-forgiveness also was found to be more difficult if the person was very empathic with the one who had been harmed. On the other hand, self-forgiveness was easier if the self-forgiver felt forgiven by the one who had been harmed or if she felt that God forgave the wrongdoing. (Hall and Fincham's description is supported in some of the work by research teams headed by Macaskill and Ross.)

Three years later, Hall and Fincham examined how self-forgiveness unfolds over time.[14] They studied US college students—not merely Christians (although in the United States, many of the students were Christians). People entered the study if they had recently harmed or offended someone and felt self-condemnation. Self-forgiveness increased over time. It often has been said that time heals all wounds. Hall and Fincham found that this was true with self-blame. But, importantly, it was not mere time that healed the wounds. Other changes were observed. As people forgave themselves and their distress decreased, they

- felt less guilty for what they had done,
- rated their wrongdoing as not as bad as they had rated it at the beginning,
- made fewer conciliatory behaviors (such as apologizing and asking for forgiveness),
- felt more forgiven by the person they had harmed, and
- felt more forgiven by and thus prayed less for help from God.

Self-blame seems to be involved with lots of internal pain. Just as slamming a cabinet door on your thumb makes you focus intently on that one thing, self-blame draws your focus to your pain. But people can get over self-blame after going to God and making things right with others. They are then able to forgive themselves, though it takes time and effort. In short, self-forgiveness occurs when you get your mind off your internal suffering and onto something more worthy of your focus, such as God or helping others.

Armed with this mini-tutorial on self-forgiveness, let's move step-by-step through the Six Steps to Self-Forgiveness. And since God is so central to the process, it makes perfect sense to start with God.

Part 3

Step 1: Receive God's Forgiveness

image of Jesus at Sacré Coeur. In that painting, Jesus is suffering, with his arms outstretched. Blood and water are flowing from his heart. Then, spiritually refueled, I would ride a bicycle to work at the Faculty of Theology. There was a beautiful English garden just outside my office—an immaculately cared for grassy area bordered by bright flowers and a hint of flowery perfume.

Colleges are where the social life of Cambridge University centers. Lectures and research take place in the faculties (which in America we call departments). So Kirby and I enjoyed the fellowship of St. Edmund's College.

In those days I thought a lot about self-condemnation. I found that Scripture has a lot to say about self-blame but not much about self-forgiveness. Scripture told me, in reference to addressing self-condemnation, that when we sin against others we also sin against God. In fact, that is so important that David wrote in Psalm 51:4, "Against you, you only, have I sinned." This was at the core of David's confession, and it is essential to us as well.

It also is important to understand that self-forgiveness is not limited to people of faith. Even atheists, in order to arrive at self-forgiveness, usually begin with the same, yet adapted, Step 1. Often they think about this step as making things right with existence or the universe—or as the step of admitting to an offense against nature or humanity.

FORGIVEN BUT FAR FROM FREE

I wanted to be free of guilt in God's eyes. I knew I had to be honest and admit to myself that I had done things that were wrong. The natural human tendency is to defend against personal guilt by denying wrongdoing, by blaming others, or by diverting attention away from guilt and focusing on our good intentions. We also are expert at excusing and jus-

7

Go to God for Understanding

The task at hand is too big to handle alone

> [God] brings us first to the end of self, to the conviction that though we have been striving to obey the law, we have failed. When we have come to the end of that, then He shows us that in the Holy Spirit we have the power of obedience, the power of victory, and the power of real holiness.
>
> —Andrew Murray

At Cambridge University, Kirby and I lived in a room at the Margaret Beaufort Institute, a charming building that is older than the United States. We still joke that our Cambridge stay was like being in Camelot. Each morning there was a brimming mud puddle in the driveway. Each afternoon it was dry. Apparently, as in Camelot, it only rained when we slept—at least in idealized memory.

At five o'clock in the morning I would tiptoe downstairs to the commons room, where I would settle in to read Christian books and the Bible, and to pray. I had time to reflect on the impact that Mike's suicide and my mother's murder had had on me. During those days I felt close to a loving God who was speaking to me.

Still reeling from Mike's death, I kept coming back to recalling the tifying our actions and twisting our motives or memories so that we see ourselves as righteous. I was all too human. Yet I knew that my heart was desperately wicked and would defend itself (see Jeremiah 17:9). So I asked God to search my heart. I confessed my sins against Mike and the results of those sins—including his inability to listen to advice that might have saved his life. I received God's forgiveness for the wrongs I had done and the things I should have done but left undone. Confession and receiving forgiveness from God are powerful, as you likely have already discovered.

The late Charles W. Colson, known as President Richard Nixon's hatchet man, served time in prison after being convicted as a conspirator to the break-in at the Watergate office complex. Technically, he was innocent of the charges. But in spirit he was far from innocent. It wasn't crime that spoiled his innocence. It was pride, which he finally faced up to after having dinner with an acquaintance, Tom Phillips, and his wife, Gert.

Tom Phillips talked frankly with Colson. "The problem with all of you, including you, Chuck—you simply had to go for the jugular.... You had to destroy your enemies because you couldn't trust in yourselves." Colson tells the story in his autobiography, *Born Again*. The conversation lit a fire under Colson. "'To myself, I admitted that Tom was on target." But outwardly, Colson defended himself with rehearsed self-justifications.

Phillips read to Colson from C. S. Lewis's classic *Mere Christianity*. Lewis wrote, "Pride leads to every other vice: it is the complete anti-God state of mind.... A proud man is always looking down on things and people: and, of course, as long as you are looking down, you cannot see something that is above you."

"Suddenly," wrote Colson, "as he [Phillips] continued [reading], one passage in particular seemed to sum up what had happened to all of us at

the White House. 'For pride is spiritual cancer: it eats up the very possibility of love, or contentment, or even common sense.'"

Colson admitted that Lewis's words described him, but he wasn't ready to make the same commitment that Phillips had made. Colson pulled out of the driveway, but then stopped his car only about one hundred yards from the Phillips's home. "With my face cupped in my hands, head leaning forward against the wheel, I forgot about machismo, about pretenses, about fears of being weak. And as I did, I began to experience a wonderful feeling of being released. Then came the sensation that water was not only running down my cheeks, but surging through my whole body as well, cleansing and cooling as it went. They weren't tears of sadness and remorse, nor of joy—but somehow tears of relief."[1]

Not Yet Free from Condemnation

As I confessed what I knew I had done wrong and received God's forgiveness, I continued to reflect. And I became aware of even more that I needed to confess. I knew that God accepted even the dark corners of my soul and the monsters that lurked within them. I rejoiced that God saved me from the penalty of my sin. But even in so doing, I did not feel peace about my failures and sins. This was troubling. I thought that sincere confession, repentance, and acceptance of God's forgiveness should cleanse me, but I didn't feel cleansed. I broached this with Kirby.

"I've been struggling," I said as we were walking to a little town near Cambridge.

"How so?" she asked.

"I've confessed my sins to God," I said, "but I can't seem to break free."

"When I have felt that way, sometimes it has helped me to ask God to show me whether there are other things I need to confess," she said.

"I'm sure there are things I haven't confessed. Yet I feel like I have examined myself, confessed, and repented. I even actually *feel* forgiven. But somehow my guilt feelings keep coming up. Until my failures around Mike's suicide, I never had such hard-to-deal-with personal failures. I had lots of sins, of course, but pretty much when I confessed and repented, I felt free. Not this time."

Scripture provides illumination

In the mornings, bundled up against the increasing perma-cold of the old building, I was reading Psalm 51. Underneath its heading was a note: "For the director of music. A psalm of David. When the prophet Nathan came to him after David had committed adultery with Bathsheba."

David's sin was such that it brought intense regret, and that part of the story is what we can identify with most readily. He had settled in as king and while Israel's army was at war, David stayed home. One night he saw Bathsheba, who was the wife of one of his generals, Uriah. She was bathing. David watched, consumed by her beauty and lusting for her. He sent for her and they slept together. She became pregnant, which worried the king since it would cause him dishonor. He brought Uriah home from the war so the military leader could spend time with his wife—an attempt by David to cover the pregnancy. But Uriah, out of honor, refused to sleep with his wife while his army remained in the field. David then issued secret orders to have Uriah put at the front of the battle and not supported. Uriah returned to the battlefield, took up a forward position, and was killed. Afterward, David took Bathsheba as a wife. He thought he had hidden his dual sins of adultery and murder (see 2 Samuel 11).

The prophet Nathan, under God's prompting, confronted David, asking for the king's judgment on a hypothetical case. Nathan told a parable that mimicked the circumstances of David's sin: a rich man with many sheep took a poor neighbor's only beloved lamb to feed the rich man's visitor. David reacted indignantly at the injustice of the situation and insisted that the thief *deserved* to die. Yet, in mercy, the king said the rich man—rather than be executed—should be required to pay four times the cost of the stolen lamb (see 2 Samuel 12:1–6). Nathan, in what has to be one of the greatest confrontations of all time, said, "You are the man!" (12:7).

The prophet then told David of God's judgment, which drew David's response: "I have sinned against the LORD." Nathan replied, "The LORD has taken away your sin" (12:13).

Cut to Psalm 51:10–12. David pleads, "Create in me a pure heart, O God, and renew a steadfast spirit within me. Do not cast me from your presence or take your Holy Spirit from me. Restore to me the joy of your salvation and grant me a willing spirit, to sustain me." But wait! If David had already confessed his wrongdoing and received God's forgiveness (see 2 Samuel 12:13), why was he still feeling cut off from God? Why was he condemning himself if God had already forgiven him? It's clear that David experienced tremendous self-condemnation *after* he was forgiven by God.

The persistence of shame

Why might self-blame and shame persist even after we receive God's forgiveness? There are spiritual and moral effects from doing wrong, but there also are social effects. God is eager to forgive us when we come humbly and ask for forgiveness on the basis of Jesus's death. Going directly to God repairs and redeems the spiritual and moral consequences of the wrongdoing. *But it does not repair the social and interpersonal consequences.* If we have damaged people and relationships through our wrongdoing, then we must try to make amends.

Take responsibility for your wrongdoing. Lewis B. Smedes, the white-haired theologian who motivated psychologists to study forgiveness by writing *Forgive and Forget,* wrote, "The hurt your heart cries hardest to forgive yourself for is the unfair harm you did to others."[2]

It is important to accept responsibility for having done wrong.

Psychologists Mickie Fisher and Julie Exline have shown this in a recent study of self-forgiveness.[3] Julie is a faculty member at Case Western Reserve University, and she has an active mind that thinks originally about topics such as forgiveness and anger toward God. Julie has practiced spiritual direction and psychotherapy. Mickie studied as Julie's graduate student early in the 2000s. She shares Julie's love of people and has honed her psychotherapy skills in clinical training.

The two psychologists conducted studies on remorse, regret, and self-forgiveness. They found that if we forgive ourselves without accepting that we have done wrong, or if we interpret our self-forgiveness to mean "I didn't do anything wrong," then we haven't really forgiven ourselves. We have simply let ourselves off the hook. That can stand in the way of handling our self-blame because it prevents us from seeking God for divine forgiveness, then apologizing and making amends to the one or ones we harmed. Also, it's nearly impossible to pretend to forgive ourselves without also accepting the weight of the harm we have done. Our unconscious mind knows when we try to take the easy way out, and it will punish us in subtle ways through guilt and shame.

Feeling the chains fall off.

I had been imprisoned by self-blame and shame. I had taken my sins to God and felt forgiven by him, yet self-condemnation still had me shackled. *Didn't I sincerely repent and feel remorse? Didn't I lay my sin at the foot of the cross? Didn't I receive God's forgiveness on the basis of Jesus's redemptive work on the cross?* I did all of these. I knew grace and mercy had taken care of my sin against Mike as well as my sins from the past, present, and future. Yet I still felt shame and self-blame, and just knowing that intensified the feelings.

When I read about King David, though, I understood that experiencing complete forgiveness from God does not remove the social effects of my sin. You might think that would be discouraging. It wasn't. It gave me something I was morally bound to do. I had to address the social consequences of sin.

Deciding to Forgive Myself

"Will you give a sermon before the Friday Guest Dinner?" asked Michael Robson, the dean of the chapel at St. Edmund's College of Cambridge. It was November, and our time in Cambridge was nearing its close. Dean Robson's request focused me on self-forgiveness. Throughout the term, I had thought, read, and prayed about it. Now, in preparing a talk, I could pull my thoughts together.

With Kirby's help, I realized I had not made an explicit decision to forgive myself. The next day in my office, I finally confronted the issue. Making a decision to forgive myself meant I would have to make some changes. I would have to stop condemning myself for being unable to make sufficient amends. I took a breath, like before diving into the deep end, and said aloud, "Okay. I choose to forgive myself. No more self-blame. The emotional self-forgiveness has got to be in God's hands. I can't make myself feel peaceful emotions."

As easy as that, I had declared my forgiveness. Questions remained. Could I follow that decision with congruent action? When? Would I ever experience emotional forgiveness and self-acceptance? That would be more of a struggle.

The Six Steps to Self-Forgiveness are not six steps that follow in a straight line or in sequential succession. My experience of forgiveness from God had taken place in a series of steps, not a once-for-all-time experience. I made a sincere decision to forgive myself, which sometimes occurs around Step 4, before completely dealing with the repair of my relationships (Step 2) or rethinking ruminations (Step 3). My decision to forgive myself did not lead me immediately to reduce my rumination (Step 3) or to REACH[4] emotional self-forgiveness (Step 4). I hoped those would come in time.

Making a decision to forgive yourself often floats from step to step. A sincere decision can empower repentance, aid the repair of relationships, help you confront unrealistic expectations, weaken rumination, and smooth the way to emotional self-forgiveness. Sometimes, though, people put off the decision or make a halfhearted decision that they must revisit in the later steps.

I felt real relief with my decision to forgive myself, but with enough residual tension to see that I wanted to continue to walk those steps. I felt the chains falling from my legs, but there was still a prison I had to escape from. Finally, though, I was running toward freedom, and it gave me a sense of elation. And with that knowledge, I felt hope replace despair.

8

Go to God with Regret, Remorse, and Repentance

The essential partnership between you and the Lord

> You do not delight in sacrifice, or I would bring it; you do not take pleasure in burnt offerings. The sacrifices of God are a broken spirit; a broken and contrite heart, O God, you will not despise.
>
> —Psalm 51:16–17

I regretted the ways I had treated Mike, the times I had been unsupportive or unavailable, the times that he crossed my mind and I promised myself I would call later, but didn't. This regret and remorse is natural, but is it a bad thing?

False Guilt Is Not Good for You

Sigmund Freud would have had people believe that false guilt is bad for us, suggesting that guilt ties up psychological energy. According to Freud, we only have so much psychological energy, or libido. To feel false guilt depletes our psychic storehouse and leaves us vulnerable to new stresses.

Freud would almost certainly have thought of my guilt as false guilt because there was nothing I could do to change my brother's suicide.

Freud, of course, formulated his theory from his psychoanalytic psychotherapy with patients. His focus was solely on his patients' psychological functioning. But what if we started with people who had not experienced a life-disruptive catastrophe?

A Psychological Study of Self-Blame

Mickie Fisher and Julie Exline,[1] introduced in the previous chapter, conducted a study on regret and remorse. They were interested in several questions, such as:

- Are people who claim to forgive themselves merely excusing their offenses?
- Might it sometimes be good for people to feel distress after they hurt others?

They found that feelings of excessive self-blame led to maladjustment, such as excessive guilt and remorse, self-condemnation, failure to accept responsibility for one's negative actions, withdrawal from social interactions, a loss of interest in others, and a variety of avoidance behaviors as a method of coping with stress. Fisher and Exline studied the difference between people who do not develop self-blame and those who do. People who did have to overcome self-blame reported more repentance and a greater sense of being humbled when they accepted responsibility and felt remorse. Reducing their negative feelings required that they exert great effort. In contrast, those who did *not* struggle with significant self-blame experienced more self-forgiveness and in turn more positive well-being, fewer negative emotions, and a more positive sense of self-esteem.

Humility and repentance were the keys to a positive reaction overall in comparison with those who were not as humble or repentant but just let themselves off the hook. Those who let themselves off the hook experienced a higher egoism and positive feelings, but they did not experience repentance and humility. They perhaps felt better, but it is uncertain whether it helped their character.

So to lower the chances that your regrettable acts and words will gnaw at you, move quickly to repent and cultivate humility. Repentance and humility are at the core of breaking free from self-blame. As they are experienced in Step 2 (Repair Relationships), they can flow out of humble repentance in one's relationship with God.

Fisher and Exline found that to be repentant and humble, people needed to do three things: (1) accept responsibility for their wrongdoing; (2) feel and show regret and remorse for what they did; and (3) realize that making up for the wrongdoing and repairing the relationship was going to be costly in time, effort, and self-sacrifice.

Repentance is actively turning away from the path you were on. To do this, you need to take responsibility, show regret and remorse, and make amends—as shown in Fisher and Exline's research. But it involves more. Repentance involves a change of heart. It requires replacing pride with humility to combat your natural tendency to defend your reputation. Humility is not merely defeating pride, just as it is not about self-abasement. Humility is thinking of others and their needs—perhaps even more than thinking about your own needs.[2]

Fisher and Exline also researched people who do *not* find a way to forgive themselves. Certain traits became evident, including egotism, avoidance of responsibility, and an excessive sense of shame. Egotism can lead to reluctance to accept responsibility. Failing to accept responsibility, in turn, can shoot self-forgiveness in the foot—and it makes it difficult for the one we harmed to forgive us as well. And even if the wronged party does forgive us, chances are good he or she won't tell us so if we refuse to take responsibility for the harm we caused.

Fisher and Exline's studies highlight what we sense from Scripture. God wants us to focus on our relationships with God and others. We are to love God above all and love our neighbor as ourselves. Scripture and science sing in harmony.

Charles Colson as an Example of Regret and Remorse

As I described earlier, Charles Colson, President Richard Nixon's general counsel, had already given his life to Jesus. Later, though, he was charged in a criminal indictment with knowing about and ordering the illegal Watergate break-ins. While he was technically innocent, he was still troubled. His newfound Christianity had become front-page headlines when he was seen going to a White House prayer breakfast. Reporters had a field day speculating about the genuineness of his faith. During an interview on *60 Minutes,* Mike Wallace grilled him. Had Colson made amends for some of his dirty political tricks? Colson couldn't answer because a public answer either way could be interpreted as an admission of illegal behavior. But Colson's sense of remorse about dirty tricks he had overseen was real, as was his desire to apologize and make amends. He was being torn apart by conflicting legal and moral demands.

> I went home that evening and fell into the deepest depression of all the dark days and nights that had gone on before. Judge Gesell had not ruled on the motions (to dismiss); he would do that later in the week, but now somehow it did not matter. Nothing he would say could alter my own self-judgment. How smug I had been during those years in the executive mansion. What happened around me never bothered me as long as I kept myself clean.... Mike Wallace's questions and the realiza-

> tion of my own crippled discipleship were pulling against me like great iron chains.... I could not shake free.[3]

After the indictments, Colson was asked to speak at a prayer breakfast in central Michigan. He prayed for the Spirit of God to speak through him. At the beginning of his talk, he felt that he owed the listeners a brief explanation of his indictments, but when he opened his mouth, he said something unexpected.

> "I know in my heart," I explained, "that I am innocent of many of the charges..."
>
> The flow of words stopped as my mind took in what I had said. "Many of the charges"— *but not all?...*
>
> My own words clinched it. My conversion would remain incomplete so long as I was a criminal defendant, tangled in the Watergate quagmire. I had to put the past behind me completely. If it meant going to prison, so be it![4]

When the trial began, Colson pleaded guilty to obstruction of justice—not something he was charged with. Judge Gesell fined him and sentenced him to one to three years in prison.

We must confront the absolute need for honesty—honesty with others, ourselves, and most of all with God. Honesty isn't a once-for-all-time event. It is ongoing. If we humbly face the truth about ourselves in relation to God and keep on embracing the truth when we are challenged, it will help prepare us for Step 2 (Repair Relationships).

Part 4

Step 2:
Repair Relationships

9

Take Responsibility

You are not the model citizen you'd like to be

> Our capacity to make peace with another person and with the world depends very much on our capacity to make peace with ourselves.
>
> —Thich Nhat Hanh

I had made a lot of progress in dealing with self-condemnation. I admitted my guilt. I confessed to God and received a measure of peace. I even granted myself decisional self-forgiveness. But I couldn't see how I could ever make amends now that Mike was dead.

God had already accepted me and forgiven me, so making amends was not a way to get in God's good graces. Instead, I wanted to make amends *because* God had forgiven me. Out of gratitude, we want to try to repair the social effects of our wrongdoing.

In the Hebrew Scriptures, we see passages that deal with making restitution (see Exodus 22:3–7; Leviticus 6:2–7). The wrongdoer makes restitution first by restoring what was wrongfully or accidently taken from the victim. Then the wrongdoer does more. If the wrongful act was an accident due to negligence, an additional one-fifth of the value is paid (see Leviticus 6). If a person intentionally robs another, the robber must pay back double (see Exodus 22). The point is not, as we know from the New Testament perspective, to adhere to the letter of these laws. Rather we must discern the principle and apply it.

Here is the principle: If I really love the person whom I have harmed, then I will want to make up for the harm I have done and, beyond that, to bless the person. This compensates for the suffering I inflicted and sends the message that I value the person.

WHAT IT TAKES TO RESTORE A RELATIONSHIP

In the movie *Something's Gotta Give,*[1] Jack Nicholson plays Harry, an immature sixty-something playboy continuously seeking affairs with young women. In the midst of one affair, he has a heart attack and, because he has to stay at the family's home to recover, he meets the young woman's mother, Erica, played by Diane Keaton. Harry is attracted to Erica, but he can't sustain a mature relationship that is appropriate for a man his age. Still, he has been changed by his fleeting experience of mature love.

He starts to seek out the young women he has used sexually, and he apologizes to each one and tries to make things right with them. Only after taking responsibility for his wrongdoing and seeking to make amends can he seek Erica's forgiveness.

Why should we make amends?

I thought this book was about forgiving oneself, you might be thinking. *How did we start talking about seeking someone else's forgiveness?* I hope you see that these two are tied intimately together. Forgiving yourself is almost always easier and sometimes possible only to the extent that you (1) accept responsibility for your wrongdoing and (2) try to make amends. (Remember Mickie Fisher and Julie Exline's research.)[2] Lots of ink has been spilled over how to forgive someone else. But almost nothing has been studied and written about how to make amends and to seek forgiveness from the person who was harmed. If you hope to forgive yourself, you must spend time and effort on that part of the process.

But psychological health and well-being are not the only reasons for making amends. Responding to God's grace and mercy requires that you try to make things right with the wronged party. Making amends also shows that you are taking responsibility.

When you harm someone, you create an injustice gap—the difference between the way a person sees the situation and the way he or she would like to see it if justice were restored. If you inflict a big injustice, you create a big injustice gap in the mind of the person you wronged. He or she will try to narrow that gap in a variety of ways—perhaps getting revenge or seeking some restitution, but also perhaps by relinquishing the issue to God. Most of us hope that the person will deal with a big injustice gap by asking for God's help. Maybe if God intervenes, we can receive mercy.

If we are struggling to forgive ourselves, then we want the person we offended to forgive us quickly. Remember Judith Hall and Frank Fincham's research.[3] They found that people could forgive themselves more quickly and thoroughly if they felt forgiven both by God and by the person they wronged.

To help the person forgive us, we can close his or her injustice gap through making amends. But we want to close the injustice gap not merely because it might hasten our ability to forgive ourselves—but so that we can forgive ourselves *responsibly.* When we hurt the other person, we damaged our own good character. To the extent that we can make amends, we narrow the sense of injustice we did to our own soul. Our responsible, restorative moral action will narrow our own injustice gap and help restore our sense of self as a moral person. That restorative justice will make it easier to forgive ourselves.

In the early 1960s, John Profumo, England's secretary of war, rocked the government by having an affair with a prostitute who had also had sex with a Soviet spy. Profumo resigned in disgrace and felt profound self-loathing. He took up work cleaning toilets at Toynbee Hall, a mission serving the destitute in the East End of London. Eventually, he was persuaded to direct the mission and continued to serve there until he died more than forty years later. Profumo couldn't make amends directly to people he harmed, so he paid it forward by dedicating himself to a life of service to the needy.

HOW A WRONGDOER CAN NARROW THE INJUSTICE GAP

To regain trust from someone you harmed, you need to show the person that you are taking full responsibility. Making amends is communication in the form of action. Think of the many times we say "sorry" out of politeness, not out of real regret. So add substance to your commitment to take responsibility by acting to narrow the injustice gap.

Usually, making amends will not completely close the gap—neither the wronged person's sense of injustice nor your own. At best, it will narrow the gap. Making amends, however, is often necessary for the wronged person. It says you are trying to bring as much justice as possible into the situation.

Why making amends is so difficult

It is difficult to make amends for many reasons. Making amends drains your energy. It is easy to give up if you aren't instantly rewarded with thanks or appreciation—which isn't likely. Also, perceptions differ. While you are making an effort to close the injustice gap, the other person may have a different motivation. As the wrongdoer, you are usually eager to make amends quickly, but the wronged party might want you to stew in your discomfort a bit—or even suffer big-time.

It is hard to balance the perceptions of the wronged person and your own perceptions of the injustice gap. The simple fact that you live inside your own skin means you feel your own pain more keenly than you feel someone else's pain. So almost always your perception of the hurt you inflicted will fall short of the intensity of the wronged person's perception. As a result, it is hard for both offender and victim ever to be equally satisfied with the wrongdoer's efforts to make restitution.

How you can succeed in making amends

I often am amazed that people can ever put transgressions behind them. I think it can be done only when at least one person is willing to be noble and altruistic, putting aside what feels like a just claim for reparations and absorbing some of the pain and suffering. The victim—if acting in mercy—can forgive and initiate reconciliation. But what is surprising is that the wrongdoer must also adopt an altruistic attitude. When we apologize and express remorse, we know how very difficult and costly that is—especially if we don't think what we did was all *that* wrong. We are keenly aware of the humiliation we feel, and we think that the other person should appreciate our sacrifice. We feel that a degree of remorse expressed and humiliation experienced should cover it.

The person we wronged, though, is usually more focused on his or her suffering—just as we are focused on our suffering. Both people need to give some grace and mercy to the other if the wound is to heal.

Most wrongdoers feel the uncomfortable emotions of guilt and maybe shame. When we experience something that is uncomfortable, our minds tell us, "End this pain. Now." But seeking to make amends keeps the wrong that we did in front of us as we try to narrow the injustice gap. Making amends also requires effort, sacrifice, humiliation, and suffering. Those are painful, of course, so we want to get it over with quickly. We rush through an apology and hope that will take care of it. The psychology of the wrongdoer is aimed at ending the episode with as little fuss as possible.

But the victim looks at things differently. The victim's psychology is shaped not by guilt and shame, but by suffering, humiliation, and pain. The wound continues to ache even after the person responsible has apologized. The psychology of the victim is shaped by regular reminders of lasting pain.

Both people can feel they are bending over backward and giving more than they are getting. This means that the only way the cycle of hurt can stop is if one or both persons are willing to make a sacrifice. One party (or both) must be willing to accept things as they are, even if he is not satisfied. In the interest of continuing a working or loving relationship, one of the persons involved can think something like, *Well, this isn't fair. But it beats holding on to the anger. I'll choose to accept the current circumstances so we can both go on with life.* As long as the two people are not in a power struggle, trying to match the number and sincerity of the apologies to the perceived harm of the wrongs that were done, this approach will work.

The practical steps of making amends

Understanding how difficult it is to satisfy both parties, you should decide on exactly what you plan to do to make amends.

First, empathize with the person you harmed, because he or she has suffered as a result. The more you understand the person's experience, the more you will be able to see the injustice gap from his or her point of view.

Second, take the initiative. Because you are the one who inflicted harm, it's up to you to take the first step toward restitution. Don't wait for the other person's complaints or coldness to motivate you to act.

Third, make restitution—and make sure it is more than you think you "ought" to make. And remember, even when you feel you are doing more than enough to make things right, it won't feel that way to the other person.

Fourth, make up your mind to sacrifice. That means you will have to let go of your sense of fairness, doing this out of love. Or if it comes to it, out of a commitment to doing what is right for the other person's benefit. Best-case scenario is that this will restore a broken relationship. And even the worst-case scenario is not so bad: you are showing the person your heart to make things right, and it is up to that person to respond.

Fifth, and perhaps most importantly, make sacrifices in silence. Be humble, and quiet, in your restitution. You must realize that even if you exceed what you feel is necessary, the other person most likely will not share your assessment. That is human nature. The other person sees his or her own suffering more clearly than yours. So be patient and loving, and try to give grace.

Going out of your way to make things right is the only path that has a realistic hope of clearing up the issue between you and the injured party. And later, that will be to your benefit in that it will make self-forgiveness more likely.

Going to God should be your first step in dealing with self-condemnation, but then move quickly to repair the social damage you caused. Only after showing that you are serious about repairing the relationship that was broken can you expect to get a good start on forgiving yourself. Don't put this off. You need to make amends near the beginning of the process of self-forgiveness, not at the end. And after that, you can begin to overcome a few more barriers. These include repairing the relationship, which begins with honest, heartfelt confession. In the next chapter, we examine how to confess.

10

Relationship Repair: The Art of Confession

Admitting you're in the wrong goes far in turning things around

> When guilt rears its ugly head confront it, discuss it and let it go. The past is over. It is time to ask what can we do right, not what did we do wrong. Forgive yourself and move on. Have the courage to reach out for help.
>
> —Bernie S. Siegel, MD

We have discussed the difficulties and the practical methods of making amends, which follows confessing your wrongdoing to God and receiving his forgiveness. Now it's time to try to repair the damaged relationship. There are direct and indirect ways to do that.

The Direct Route to Relationship Repair

The straightest line to repairing a relationship is to go directly to the person and confess your wrongdoing. Be wise about this. Bear in mind that it's not always the best first thing to try, and at times it is not even possible. In our litigious society, confessing a wrong might lead to a lawsuit or unjust court settlements against you. And often, if the act you are confessing dates back some years, the person might have moved away and cut off contact. Or in my case, a brother might have committed suicide.

When the direct approach works, it can be liberating. A symbolic, award-winning photograph from the Vietnam War, taken by Huynh Cong "Nick" Ut, was published in June 1972. It shows a naked girl screaming in pain from being splashed in napalm as her village burns in the background. How can a young girl stand such pain? Surely, suffering the anguish of an attack of this nature would bring bitterness and hatred—especially of the perpetrators of such evil.

The girl in the photograph was Pham Thi Kim Phuc. It took seventeen operations to restore her to some semblance of health. Later, Kim moved to Toronto and has become a public speaker. In 1996 she spoke at a Veterans Day event in Washington, DC. She told the audience, "Even if I could talk face to face with the pilot who dropped the bombs, I would tell him we cannot change history but we should try to do good things for the present and for the future to promote peace."[1] John Plummer was sitting in the audience that day.

Plummer felt responsible, saying he had arranged the raid on Kim's village, though later events cast some doubt on the accuracy of his statement. The day before Kim's talk, he had opened the newspaper to stare at the horror of his handiwork—the photo of Kim as a child. From June 1972 to 1996, Plummer had stewed in guilt and shame. In 1996 he said, "It just knocked me to my knees. And that was when I knew I could never talk about this." Plummer did what we often do with shame—he tried to bury it. *Tried* is the best word for this, because shame is like a zombie. Guilty memories fight their way out of the graves we dig for them. They stalk us with outstretched arms and decomposed fingers that grasp at our hearts. Plummer said that, since 1972, he'd had nightmares of the village's children crying.

When he saw that Kim was scheduled to speak in Washington, DC, he made arrangements to attend the event, where he met with her and apologized. "It's all right," Kim said gently. "I forgive. I forgive." Despite some question regarding Plummer's claim of responsibility for the mission, Kim was gracious to forgive and to seek to repair the relationship.[2] At its best, the direct approach to relationship repair can be life changing.

The Indirect Approach to Relationship Repair

The second route to making amends is an indirect approach. It's the only path left when we can't contact and meet with the person who was harmed or offended—perhaps because he or she is not available or is no longer alive. Or possibly because it would be dangerous to meet with the person. Instead, we do things that are socially beneficial on behalf of the person harmed. In my case, I could not repair the damage I had done to my brother. But I held out hope that someday I could do something to make up for my failures.

At the Chautauqua Institution in 2005, I had said I hoped I would learn enough from my experience of self-blame to help others. Teaching others how to enter into the freedom of self-forgiveness would be an indirect way to make amends.

President Clinton's intern scandal

President Bill Clinton almost brought down the presidency with his sexual liaisons with intern Monica Lewinsky. Clinton eventually made amends, and because he was the president, his wrongdoing was made public and was analyzed and discussed for years.

Clinton had engaged in sexual liaisons with Lewinsky in 1995 and

1996, finally breaking off the relationship early in 1997. He described the affair and the aftermath in his book *My Life: The Presidential Years, Volume II.*

When Lewinsky began talking to a coworker, Linda Tripp, Tripp recorded the conversations. She brought the tapes to the attention of Kenneth Starr, the head investigator looking into the alleged wrongdoings of Bill and Hillary Clinton. Rumors flew about the Tripp tapes. Bill Clinton, writing in retrospect, said his initial approach was to deny what happened to everyone involved.

He was friends with South Africa's president, Nelson Mandela, who had been imprisoned for twenty-seven years by that nation's apartheid regime. Clinton described what Mandela once said to him during a time of Clinton's anguish over his own misdeeds. Clinton asked whether Mandela had ever hated his oppressors:

> Of course, I did, for many years.... Then one day when I was working in the quarry, hammering the rocks, I realized that they had already taken everything from me except my mind and my heart. Those they could not take without my permission. I decided not to give them away.[3]

Eventually, Clinton fessed up to his misdeeds and deceptions. On August 15, 1998, he was two days away from appearing before a grand jury to testify under oath. It was time to come clean. He told Hillary and their daughter, Chelsea, about his meetings with Lewinsky and admitted that he had lied to them.

After testifying to the grand jury, the president decided to confess to the American people. At the beginning of his confession, he stated that he was taking responsibility for his actions. But as he continued his comments, he made excuses and justified his acts on the basis of his anger at the Starr Commission for its bulldog-like investigation and having to deal with his personal crisis at a time of national crisis and threat involving al-Qaeda. The apology did not go down well with the American people. He had contaminated his apology with self-justification and by blaming his critics. More would be required to show that he truly was taking personal responsibility. Clinton was a sincere Christian, and he had committed himself to definite steps of amends-making. Months later, on March 3, 1999, he stated his intentions publicly. He and Hillary were hosting the National Prayer Breakfast, which welcomed governmental and religious leaders who came together in Washington. Clinton addressed the assembly. "I don't think there is a fancy way to say that I have sinned," he began.

> I said that I was sorry for all who had been hurt—my family, friends, staff, cabinet, and Monica Lewinsky and her family; that I had asked for their forgiveness and that I would pursue counseling from pastors and others to find, with God's help, a willingness to give the very forgiveness I seek, a renunciation of the pride and the anger which cloud judgment, lead people to excuse and compare and to blame and complain.[4]

Clinton described the counseling he received from three pastors and the advice provided by other wise Christians. He talked of receiving couple counseling with Hillary, and understanding the impact of certain childhood experiences and the poor decisions he had made in the past as an adult. He said that he now understood how vulnerable he was when he was tired, angry, and isolated.

Consider that Clinton stood before the American people and made some of the most shameful disclosures any person could make. Much of his amends-making, as well, became public. He didn't just try to undo the wrong and move on. He apologized and asked for forgiveness repeatedly, and he sought counseling so that he could experience responsible self-forgiveness. While he made direct attempts to repair his relationship with his wife and daughter, he could only follow indirect means with Monica Lewinsky and with the people of the United States, whose trust he had violated. Through making costly personal and public admissions, he sought to undo some of the harm he was responsible for and to restore some semblance of trust to a damaged presidency.

THE ART OF A GOOD CONFESSION

Clinton's first public confession bombed because it was tainted by self-justifications, blame of others, and anger. His second confession—at the National Prayer Breakfast—came a lot closer to being an effective confession. That time, he sounded sincere when he referred to his remorse and regret. And by seeking to make amends through entering couple and individual counseling, he was acting on his words. He also addressed all of the injured parties and tried to do what he could to apologize to them and seek their forgiveness.

Most of us will never have the opportunity (and for that we are most thankful) to apologize for misdeeds under the glare of the news media and political enemies. Mostly, our apologies are between us and one person. When we talk with that person, a sequence of events often happens.

The wronged person makes a *reproach.* A reproach is the person's request that we explain why we committed a wrong against him or her. We then give an account of our behavior. We can make an unhelpful account, such as denying that we did wrong or justifying what we did, usually with an excuse such as saying that the other person was at least partly responsible. We could even make a clumsy excuse, listing a number of mitigating reasons for our harmful behavior (I was tired or I was misunderstood or I didn't mean it the way it came out or I had a headache). *Or* we could make a legitimate confession.

Eight parts to a good confession

A good confession has seven parts.[5]

The wrongdoer first must confess the wrong acts without excuse. Then apologies are in order. It is wise to show that you, the wrongdoer, empathize with the person hurt. You also assure the person that he or she is valued. An offer of restitution—making up for harm done, and then some—can help heal the relationship. It helps also if you assure the person that all effort will be made to prevent a similar hurt from ever happening again. Finally, make an explicit request for forgiveness.

Here is a bare-bones outline of a good confession. Suppose that I work late, completely forgetting my anniversary. Kirby has prepared a candlelit dinner. By the time I get home, the special dinner is overcooked and the veggies are cold. The fruit is brown and the sparkling apple juice has lost its sparkle.

As I walk through the door, I smell great food, see fine dishes set out on our best tablecloth. And I see the burned-down candles.

Uh-oh, I think.

"I thought you said this morning that you'd be home at six," says Kirby.

"I did, and I'm so sorry I'm late." (It is tempting to immediately offer an excuse, such as "I got involved in work and didn't notice the time," or even try to shift a bit of the blame by saying, "I saw I was going to be late and I phoned, but the phone was busy." Neither would be a good strategy.)

"I am late, and especially on our anniversary, that's inexcusable. I really am sorry. I see that you've worked hard to make this meal special. Now I've messed it up. I know you must be hurt, angry, and sad. I feel terrible. I love you. I hope there can be some way to make it up to you. I hate that I hurt and disappointed you. I am going to try my hardest never to be late on an anniversary or birthday again. Can you forgive me?"

RESPONSES TO A CONFESSION

The offended person will not simply gush with forgiveness and reconciliation. At least, not right away. So think back to the psychology of transgressions. The offender usually asks for forgiveness before the victim is willing to grant it. But that poses a problem. If the victim values the relationship, she won't want to flat-out refuse to forgive. But she also doesn't want to blurt out a quick "I forgive you." To get back to the example of my lateness on our anniversary, I must be sensitive to the bind I put Kirby in. It is unrealistic to demand quick forgiveness just because I gave a good confession.

But what if the other person refuses to grant forgiveness? The person could say, "Absolutely not! You've gone too far this time. I will never forgive you." That will hamper future interactions, far beyond discussions of the matter at hand. More likely, the person will say, "I cannot forgive you *yet.*" The person might need to think about your confession before being willing to grant forgiveness. But "I cannot forgive you *yet*" also can mean your confession failed to meet the standards of a good-enough apology. Or it could mean you didn't offer to make sufficient restitution. The injustice gap is still too wide.

"Not yet" also can mean that the person might have made a decision to forgive, but he or she still is upset. It will take time before the person's emotions change enough that he or she feels that forgiveness has taken place.

It is important for the offender not to get hurt by a "not yet" response. After an emotionally costly confession, the offender wants the victim to understand how hard it was to admit the wrongdoing. The offender at that point is focused on the difficulty of having made himself vulnerable and exposed. But that does not mean the wronged party will quickly be able to forgive.

The offender must give the person time and space. It takes time for the offended person to be able to forgive. Think about a time when you were hurt by someone. How long did it take you to offer genuine forgiveness? To say, "I forgive you," is a big step, and before taking that step most people want to see hard evidence that real repentance has taken place.

HAVE OTHER PEOPLE BEEN HURT?

Often your wrongdoing has a negative impact on the lives of more than just the person you offended. If a husband has an affair, it harms his wife and also his children, the in-laws, and his own parents. He might need to apologize to many people. He must consider others when deciding how to make amends. There are people in the church who feel betrayed and those outside the church who feel justly judgmental when someone in the church falls into immorality. Wrongdoing, when it becomes public, can strain friendships and even working relationships. As we think about making amends, we have to ask hard questions about how far we must go to make amends. When you confess to the Lord a wrong you committed, you might feel moral freedom because you know that Jesus died for your sin. But your obligation to repair the social harm you have done extends to the affected parties, and it is wise to consider each one.

I wanted to make amends for my years of failing to love and respect my brother and—near the end of his life—my failure to help him. But at Cambridge, I could see nothing that I could do. Then something opened up that I could never have predicted.

Make Amends Through Responsible Compassion

Thinking of others can help you make things right

> In community. . .God's compassion becomes present in the midst of a broken world.
>
> —Henri Nouwen

In Cambridge I had sought forgiveness from God and then made a decision to forgive myself. Yet I had not experienced much emotional forgiveness. The decision to forgive myself had taken some of the emotional pressure off and I felt better, but still I was not at peace.

Contributing to my unsettled feeling was the suicide note Mike had addressed to me. I had not yet obtained the note from the Oak Ridge, Tennessee, police. The thought of facing my brother's condemnation, and knowing that the words in the note were the last things he had expressed, was too threatening. Since his death, I had done little else but rebuke myself for my failures. And in the back of my mind, it seemed that Mike would have added his own criticisms to mine.

Back home from England, Kirby and I took her mother, who had advancing dementia, for a three-week stay in South Florida. After returning her to Atlanta, Kirby and I started home to Virginia.

"We're three hours from Knoxville," I said as we headed to the interstate. "We should visit Charlene." We agreed to take the side trip, and we had a good talk with our sister-in-law. She was coping well. David was living elsewhere after graduating from high school. Then Charlene mentioned that the Oak Ridge police still had the suicide note.

I would like to say that I went to the police station and demanded they hand over the note. I wish I could add that I tore it open and read it aloud, honestly and boldly facing up to whatever it was that my brother had left behind for me to see. But instead, I still lacked the courage to read what Mike had written. I let Kirby and Charlene retrieve the note. When they returned, Kirby handed me a sealed envelope. My hands were shaking. Finally, I slipped a finger beneath the seal.

The note said this:

> Ev, I know that you will keep your head in this crisis. I left our finances in disarray. I am concerned that Charlene will not be able to straighten them out after I'm gone. Will you straighten out our finances?

I stared, dumfounded, at my brother's note. No rebuking. No wild rage at my betrayal. No blame. Not even gentle chiding. Just a plea for help. My first thought was relief. *Thank you, God,* I thought. *Mike has given me something to do!* In a voice from the grave, Mike had given me something positive to do. I could help Charlene and David, just as he had asked me to do.

The Necessity of Reconciliation

I shared this story a few years later at a conference. As I stood in line at a sandwich shop after the conference had ended, a woman rose from her table and walked my way. "I was in the audience this morning," she said. "I've been thinking about your brother's note. Maybe it wasn't just a way for you to make up for not helping him. His letter, in effect, said, 'I trust you. Our relationship has not been so damaged that I don't trust you.' You said that reconciliation is the 'restoration of trust after trust has been violated.' His letter said that he felt—no matter how dark his end time was—that you and he had been reconciled."

Hot tears fell from my eyes. Standing in line, near a sandwich-shop counter with potato salad and chips in my hands, I wept like a child.

Reconciliation doesn't have to mean that a relationship takes on a new, conflict-free dynamic. Like Jacob and Esau, though their relationship was reconciled, they did not continue to live as neighbors (see Genesis 33:16–20).[1] They went different ways and raised their families apart from each other. Maybe Mike had felt reconciled after all.

WHY SELF-BLAME IS SO HARD TO FACE

I admit that I put off reading the suicide note because of pride. I believed in my heart—regardless of how much I might disavow it outwardly—that I could not trust God to protect me. Rather, I had to protect myself. But God is fully able to protect us without our assistance.

Even before Mike's death, before I started the six steps, before I began to repair my troubled relationships, God was protecting me with compassion, using others as willing instruments to encourage me.

Self-forgiveness is private. You can do it anywhere, just you alone with God. But the context for forgiving yourself is interpersonal. You wronged someone, otherwise you would not feel the need to forgive yourself. You know now that you must make amends. When you decide to forgive yourself, that first step helps you then to take the step of making amends.

When others help and encourage us, that often is the thing that makes it possible to forgive ourselves. Throughout my journey, Kirby has been my constant help. More than anyone else, she has helped me get my focus off myself and onto other people. But before my journey is done—if journeys are ever done—you'll see others who came alongside me.

WHY REACH OUT TO OTHERS?

If you are at all sensitive to others, you will see the pain you have caused them. You will want to help the person you offended —not just out of guilt, but because you connect empathically. You get into his or her frame of mind. From there, you can see what the person needs and how that will help repair the relationship. However, by empathizing, you also do what is far less obvious. You become more connected emotionally with the person. You start to feel sympathy, compassion, or even love toward the person. When that happens, the other person can sense it. Your relationship will get markedly better.

Also, your heart can sense it. Psychologist Stephanie Brown and her colleagues from the University of Michigan conducted a prospective study.[2]

Prospective studies are those in which people are measured at an initial point of testing and then followed to see which subjects develop difficulties, which ones show resiliency, and which ones develop exceptional strengths years later. Brown and her team looked closely at how much and what type of social support each subject had.

For decades, psychotherapists and counselors have known that receiving the right type of social support at a time of need can be helpful. Of interest here is that Brown and her colleagues found that *providing* social support to those who need it can be at least as beneficial to the provider as receiving social support is for the recipient.

Barbara L. Fredrickson, a researcher now at the University of North

Carolina at Chapel Hill, originated what is perhaps the most quoted idea in the positive psychology movement: the broaden-and-build theory of positive emotions.[3]

Positive emotions broaden our outlook and build our resources. Negative emotions focus our attention on survival, expending resources simply to survive. Fredrickson and her colleagues, in their Open Heart Study, had people practice loving-kindness meditation regularly. Loving-kindness meditation involves thinking loving thoughts about God, others, and oneself. It also can be used to pray for others or meditate on the kindness and compassion one has received or hopes to show to others. Fredrickson's team found that when people practiced loving-kindness, they not only felt more warmth and caring, but they also increased their care and support for other people. Both were associated with better health and building personal resources.

This suggests that if we have harmed someone, then the preparation for making amends includes thinking kind, warm, and caring thoughts about the person or praying often for the person's welfare. This serves to change our attitude toward the person, and it also could change our behaviors toward that person—thus helping the person. And, as a bonus, beaming loving-kindness toward someone could reflect back and produce improved health and well-being in us.

The physical and psychological effects of sincere, loving prayer—beyond the spiritual effects in asking God for help in restoring the relationship—could help heal both individuals and the relationship.

THE IMPORTANCE OF OTHERS

Psychological science is singing a song from the wisdom of ages in religion and philosophy. Other people are crucial if we are to break free from self-condemnation. Focusing on ourselves and our suffering escalates self-blame and shame. Focusing on helping others leads to healing. It is very possible that at one time we identified the other person as having provoked our misdeed, and even that the person prolonged his injustice toward us by triggering our self-condemning thoughts. But the other person also can be the target of our empathy, compassion, care, and love—and a recipient of our help.

Literally coming alongside

Back in Richmond, Virginia, I was outdoors and walking fast, about five miles from home. I passed a woman striding energetically in the other direction, and suddenly she reversed herself. "You're a runner, aren't you?" she asked. I said yes, and she began to talk. She lamented no longer being able to run marathons and cried because her husband didn't understand her. As we talked, I gave her some marital advice. She was a complete stranger.

As we parted, I thought, *A stranger suddenly appears and confides personal details about her life. And why did she tell* me—*who studied and wrote about marriage and forgiveness—about the very topics I know something about?* Then I realized I was wearing a baseball cap with a Richmond Marathon logo. She had seen the logo and thought of me as a kindred spirit. She thought I would appreciate her great love of running and see the impact of her not being able to run marathons.

Here's the irony. I've *never* run in a marathon. Kirby got the cap for me at a yard sale. I felt like such a fraud. That feeling, though, was short-lived. I realized that God had seen that a woman needed help with her struggles. So God took a marriage counselor and forgiveness researcher, and dressed him in a Richmond Marathon cap so that he could be easily recognized. Then God allowed me to walk alongside a woman to share what wisdom I had to offer.

This is often the way healing takes place. God steps into history and dresses us up so that we can easily be recognized as helpers. We walk with people until some healing has occurred. Then we go our separate ways.

As often as not, we are the ones who need someone to come alongside us. We are the ones who must look to others to see the divine help God is providing through even the seemingly unlikely people who come across our paths. We receive help from unexpected sources—people whom we think *we* are helping. God loves us enough to send messengers of his love until the meaning of the messages sink in.

I Finally Could Make Amends

Early in 2006 I started straightening out the family finances for Charlene and her son, which took a few months. Eventually I got their bonds cashed in and the taxes worked out. I distributed the funds of my mother's estate.

And for the next several months, I threw myself into my work. I worked out the six steps I am describing in this book. I began to understand what my emotional experience had been during the year since Mike's suicide.

I had come a long way. I had confessed my failures to God and accepted forgiveness. I had seen the importance of others and had made some amends. I had forgiven myself. Yet I still struggled with *emotionally* forgiving myself and with fully accepting myself. Because I was pressured with demands from work, it was easy to ignore the necessary work of aligning my emotions and self-acceptance with a decision to forgive myself. It was as if I had broken free of the manacles of self-blame but I got sidetracked after getting out of the cell. I felt as if I were still wandering around in a dungeon, through a dark maze. I didn't realize then that the forces that kept me in the dark were ruminations and unrealistic expectations. Let's first take a look at ruminations.

Part 5

Step 3: Rethink Ruminations

12

Struggles with God

Sometimes we feel it's necessary to wrestle with the Almighty

> Others are mirrors in which we are constrained to see ourselves, not as we would like to be, but as we are.
>
> —Mike Mason, *The Mystery of Marriage*

For a few rare people, self-forgiveness happens all at once. Suddenly a person sees something that changes her view of herself. The turning point gives her a completely new perspective on her past and the life ahead, and that event transforms her. She is released into miraculous freedom.

For other people, forgiveness happens step-by-halting-step. It is like climbing a mountain. There are periods of steep trudging; paths that follow a narrow, perilous route along the edge of a cliff; brief periods of walking downhill; beautiful vistas; dark cedar corridors; and finally climbing over boulders at the summit.

For others, self-forgiveness arrives almost without being noticed. It's a gradual erosion of self-blame and the slow evaporation of shame. These people don't notice a big emotional event. They seem to wake up one day and realize that their self-blame and shame have dissipated.

For me, it was a step-by-step process. My progress was anything but uniform or quick. During the fall of 2006, I was immersed in work and chose to not think about my ongoing struggle.

A WAKE-UP CALL

Then in January 2007, I attended a research-group meeting at Biola University. This group has met annually since 2001 to discuss issues in Christianity and psychology, and at times to plan research together. The speaker that year was Maureen Miner from Australia. Maureen takes a psychoanalytic approach to religion and psychology, and she studies attachment to God. She presented some of her research on the first night. Afterward, back at the hotel, she and I happened to get off the elevator at the same floor. We stood in the elevator lobby talking. She asked about my current work on forgiveness.

"I'm most excited about research on self-forgiveness by my doctoral student, Katie Campana," I said. "I have been thinking for the last few years about self-blame and shame. I struggled with them for the first year after my brother's death. I made some progress, but life goes on."

Maureen said, "Yes, I heard that your mother had been murdered."

"My brother, Mike, found her body. He never could get the images of the murder scene out of his mind. At times, evil seems to get the upper hand. The one who killed my mother got a two-for-one. Mike suffered for ten years, then killed himself."

"It sounds as if it really affected you," said Maureen.

"Well, I've worked through parts of it, but I'm stuck now."

"How so?"

"My spiritual life has gotten dry. I get up at five every morning, get my coffee, and look at the Bible or Christian books I could read. Then I usually do work instead. I'm under a lot of pressure at work. It seems that the only way to get out from under it is to use that early-morning time for work."

Maureen listened attentively, as a good psychotherapist does. Theologian Paul Tillich once said, "The first duty of love is to listen."[1] As I talked and Maureen listened, I could hear my own words as if I were an outside observer. I heard bitterness when I talked about Mike's death, and worse, when I mentioned my relationship with God.

I walked to my room thinking, *I sounded so bitter. I've forgiven that young man* [who killed my mother], *but that bitterness sounded like I had all but abandoned God.*

I cry easily at touching stories and movies and sometimes in joy, but when I have reason to feel sad about developments in my own life, I almost never cry. That night, though, I broke down. I walked away from the hallway conversation grateful to Maureen for listening and grateful that I had heard my own bitterness. I knew now I might be able to do something about it.

But what?

As I pondered the state of my spirit, the puzzle fell into place. It went back to my family of origin, where I had learned to withdraw from conflict. My parents used to argue over Dad's drinking. To avoid the tension and conflict, I would go to the cold back bedroom to work math problems. By pursuing academic achievement, I could remove myself physically from their conflict. By getting into school leadership, I could avoid going home right when classes ended. Withdrawal and achievement became my major coping mechanisms.

In 2007, I was repeating a familiar pattern. Realizing then that I had been withdrawing into work, I started looking for the conflict that was motivating me to hide. It could be only one thing: I was battling God.

I couldn't understand why my younger brother was dead. I couldn't understand why the traumas we had had in our family were so difficult. I could not get any kind of answer to the questions—though I never admitted even struggling with the questions. After Mike's suicide, if I had been asked whether I was in conflict with God, I would have said, "Absolutely not. I don't ever question God." And consciously I did not doubt my faith. Yet when I found myself alone with my thoughts, the doubts and questions would run wind sprints across my mind. I would crush them because I felt that doubts and questions indicated anemic faith. But the unacknowledged struggle with God was moving me further from God. I was running toward work to avoid dealing with God.

This is my story, of course. But aspects of it might roughly parallel your own experience. Struggling with God is common, but it is not a required part of forgiving yourself. All I can say is that for me, it was crucial. I was using workaholism and perfectionism to try to silence my urge to get in the cage with God and have it out. Gloves off, no holds barred. Just me and God, bare knuckles, where we would settle this thing here and now.

When I finally admitted this to myself, it opened other areas in which I needed to forgive myself. First, I was striving for perfection and acceptance through achievement in my work. Second, I felt guilt over my lingering resentment toward God.

I knew I could repair my estranged relationship with God. I had drifted from God before, and always God has been faithful to me. But I needed an effective strategy if I was going to win the battle over bitterness toward God and my inability to emotionally forgive myself.

The problem was, I didn't have a clue what an effective battle plan would look like.

Recognizing Life "in the Flesh"

Time passed and still I had no strategy. By December 2007, occupied with the responsibilities of life, I felt less distress over Mike's death and my failings. Yet in reflective times, I had to admit I still was withdrawn from God. In spite of my wake-up call when talking to Maureen Miner months earlier, I felt like I was now wandering even further from home. For one thing, my workload had cranked up another notch. I was far too overcommitted.

God had given me a life mission during the 1990s after my mother's murder: I was to do all I could to bring forgiveness into every willing heart, home, and homeland. Whenever a college, church, or civic organization asked me to speak, I said yes (unless the time was already obligated). But I realized that I had let my mission become an idol.

Blaise Pascal, in the *Pensées,*[2] said, "The heart has its reasons, which reason cannot know." My heart had pursued safety from pain through the distraction of work. I needed to reorient myself toward God. I was working "in the flesh," meaning I was relying on my own efforts instead of resting in God. In Romans 8:6, Paul wrote: "To set the mind on the flesh is death, but to set the mind on the Spirit is life and peace" (NRSV). I wasn't feeling any peace. Instead of being centered on Jesus, I was following my life mission in an unhealthy and ungodly way. As I withdrew from conflict with God, I was being shoved to the outer reaches of a relationship with God. I knew I should fight against the current, but I was resisting even that impulse to act.

Open Eyes

I was overwhelmed. I awoke from sleep during my "devotional time" early one morning and pulled out a psychology book I needed to read. I thought, *My devotions have become a devotion to reading things other than God's Word.* Suddenly I was shaken by the realization that I still was held in the prison of self-condemnation. I had cast off the immediate chains, but I could see that I was in increasing danger of entering again a locked cell.

I went to my bedroom and retrieved Malcolm Muggeridge's *Confessions of a Twentieth-Century Pilgrim.*[3] He quoted a fragment from a statement made by Aleksandr Solzhenitsyn. Here is the more extended version containing the oft-quoted gem that evil passes through every human heart:

> It was only when I lay there on rotting prison straw that I sensed within myself the first strivings for good. Gradually, it was disclosed to me that the line separating good and evil passes not through states, nor between classes, nor between political parties either—but right through every human heart—and through all human hearts. This line shifts. Inside us, it oscillates with the years. And even within hearts overwhelmed by evil, one small bridgehead of good is retained. And even in the best of hearts, there remains...an unuprooted small corner of evil. Since then I have come to understand the truth of all religions of the world: They struggle with the evil inside a human being (inside every human being). It is impossible to expel evil from the world in its entirety, but it is possible to constrict it within each person.[4]

I realized that inside me, in *this* human being, I was not trying to constrict the evil of self-absorption, which had been pulling me away from God. Quite the opposite: I was indulging it. It had taken over a corner of my heart due to my pattern of withdrawing from conflict. I knew it would take over my heart if it were not halted. I needed to do something to reverse its spread.

I prayed. I knew there was no solution without the Lord's help. And I knew that much of the solution had to do with changing my unrealistic expectations and standards.

FINALLY, A PLAN OF ACTION

I know from doing clinical research and therapy with thousands of clients that I am not alone in battling unrealistic expectations and standards. The details of my story won't match yours, but the pressures and our reaction to the pressures often bear a remarkable similarity. We are hard on ourselves. We expect ourselves to be better and stronger than we are. We enforce standards on ourselves that we would never apply to others—because somehow we feel we should always rise to the challenges.

So my story most likely has important lessons for you, to be applied to the particulars of your own struggle. In my case, I had always lost myself in work and achievement. I needed to find a more normal motivation for achievement to replace my drivenness to achieve. To do this, I needed to

1. change my standard,
2. change my performance,
3. commit to closing the gap, and
4. cease striving for perfection and instead bring my failures to God.

As a first step I started to use my early-morning devotion times to think and pray about how to strengthen my relationship with God.

Changing unhealthy standards

I had to stop my tendency to withdraw from conflict. Lately, this self-protective and mindless habit had kept me estranged from God. God was not an unpredictable earthly father who often was drunk, argumentative, and emotionally harsh. But even knowing that, I realized that changing my lifelong pattern of withdrawal was not going to be easy.

When Kirby and I were first married, I tried to withdraw whenever we had conflicts. Fortunately, Kirby kept lovingly insisting that we talk things out. We did, and that was an important break between my past and the type of person I could become. Understanding that I had fallen into the same destructive pattern with God was a good first step forward. I needed to whip my reliance on withdrawal.

Changing my performance

The second related problem was to stop distracting myself with work. I knew that distraction from God would not strengthen my relationship with God. I had proven that over the past couple of years. I had to defeat distraction—in my case, my mission and my work—so I could carve out time for God. If I was to work things out with God, there had to be a place where we would meet regularly. I had to protect my five-to-seven time every morning for God alone.

Committing to closing the gap

I reconsidered my mission statement. If my mission was "to do all I can to promote forgiveness...," I knew there would always be more and more that I could do. I had to use discernment, which required seeking the leading of the Holy Spirit in making decisions about what I did, and didn't, need to do. I decided I would not allow my teaching, my academic research, or any other facet of my work to intrude on my two-hour time for devotions every day.

Each morning I read for thirty to forty-five minutes. Then I would journal, pray, and reflect on how things might be made better between God and me. My preference for distraction and withdrawal were patterns that came from my flesh. In Romans 8, Paul wrote that following the flesh leads to death. The sinful pattern of withdrawing from God, the One I needed most, had to be rooted out. Only Christ can set us free, so I turned back to him.

Stop striving for perfection

I had to deal with my perfectionism, which was showing up primarily through intense self-blame and increasing workaholism and a drive for achievement. It was as if I believed that shoring up my superior self-image would, perhaps, enable me to avoid facing my woundedness. I still blamed myself for not being able to forgive myself emotionally and reach a place of peace. It had been almost three years since Mike's suicide. I felt like I ought to be over this.

SATAN, SIN, AND SELF

I was ready to go to war against my self-defeating expectations. A careful analysis of the situation showed that the problems fell into three areas, all of which apply to each one of us. First, I had an unhealthy reliance on withdrawal and distraction—relying on myself and my failed reliance on evasive actions. Second, I needed to employ discernment and overcome perfectionism and workaholism—in other words, to overcome destructive sinful patterns. And third, I had to come to terms with my battle against God—and in doing so, to resist the distractions and influence of Satan. Christians at all levels of maturity struggle with these three: self, sin, and Satan.

Satan had been telling me I had done unforgivable wrongs in my treatment of Mike as we were growing up. Satan added that I was a bad person now for struggling with God. Sin was manifested by my continued inability to live a life of faith, choosing instead to seek false safety in my choice to withdraw. And my entire self was involved through setting and attempting to reach personal standards that, by any objective measure, were far too high to attain.

Satan, sin, and self are the sources of your problems as well as mine.

Any one of them, or all three, can produce a false sense of guilt. Satan is the accuser (see 1 Peter 5:8–9; Revelation 12:10). If I listen to his accusations, they will make me feel guilty. The demands of my fallen flesh also can give rise to false guilt. If I want to avoid pain and show myself that I am worthwhile, then sin (in the form of the demands of the flesh) can lead to false guilt. And to compound the problems, the demands of the human spirit—or the self—can lead to a sense of false guilt.

Our own standards are a faulty measure and one that is guaranteed to feed our frustration, disappointment, and bitterness. Our inability to achieve a level of perfection that we set for ourselves can result in self-blame and overwhelming shame. The cycle feeds on itself. We can't reach the standards because we set the standards too high.

Let's take a look at why we do this.

13

How to Adjust Perfectionistic Standards and Unrealistic Expectations

Getting real about yourself moves the process forward

> The past is never dead. It's not even past.
>
> —William Faulkner

Step 3 in the Six Steps to Self-Forgiveness is to rethink your ruminations. Ruminations come in a couple of flavors. Some focus on obsessing about negative things in your life—wallowing in your regrets, mentally regurgitating past failures that make you ill just to think about them. Other ruminations center on failures to live up to your standards. Just because no one else is perfect doesn't mean that you can't achieve perfection. Right? Wrong.

It's time to recognize and replace your unrealistic expectations and limit the messages you send to yourself that make you miserable. The downward spiral of your ruminations is fueled by unrealistic expectations and out-of-reach standards. I can identify family members and my personal history that influenced my unrealistic standards. But you were influenced by different forces and a different personal history. Still, we all can identify causes from the past and the present that influenced our overly high standards and unrealistic expectations.

INFLUENCES FROM THE PAST

Any number of influences from the past can push you to strive for too much and thus become a leading candidate for failing. You might believe messages from your childhood that no longer apply to your life; you might accept lies as being true; you might have overlooked spiritual strongholds; and you might be convinced, in advance, that you will fail.

Messages that no longer apply

When we are children, we think as children. Sometimes that thinking has a magical quality that we would love to recapture in adulthood. Other times, however, we develop early beliefs that maintain an unhealthy grip on our adult lives. For example, we develop attachments and behavior patterns that made perfect sense to a preschool-age child. But as adults, we must recognize and control those unconscious patterns. According to Freud, we must exert ego control over the made-in-the-past impulses and conflicts. And according to Paul, we must take every thought captive for Christ (see 2 Corinthians 10:5).

Psychotherapists know it does little good to point out a person's pattern of deep-seated misconceptions rooted in childhood experiences. Instead, people usually must discover the patterns for themselves. Then they must be helped to (1) recognize what triggers their automatic behavior, (2) be motivated to change the behavior, and (3) come to believe they can change the behavior.

Believing lies

In John 8:44, Jesus told his enemies: "You belong to your father, the devil, and you want to carry out your father's desire. He was a murderer from the beginning, not holding to the truth, for there is no truth in him. When he lies, he speaks his native language, for he is a liar and the father of lies." Satan will lie to you in different ways. You can believe, for instance, that you did something so terrible that you should not even confess it to God, much less to others. You can believe that no sacrifice (not even Jesus's death) could pay for the evil you have done. You also can believe that the person you hurt has been irreparably damaged and it would do no good to attempt to make amends. These lies are calculated to keep you stuck in patterns of intractable self-blame.

Not considering spiritual strongholds

In his second letter to the Corinthians, Paul confronted people who had told lies about him. They had created a stronghold, behind which they were sniping at and criticizing Paul. Paul wrote a letter to the church in that city, using a battle metaphor to describe how he intended to deal with those who would be his enemies and the enemies of God.

However, there appears to be a second level of communication going on as well. Paul often wrote that "Our struggle is not against flesh and blood, but against...the powers of this dark world and against the spiritual forces of evil in the heavenly realms" (Ephesians 6:12). It appears that Paul was talking also about spiritual forces that are arrayed behind and around our flesh-and-blood foes. He wrote:

> The weapons we fight with are not the weapons of the world. On the contrary, they have divine power to demolish strongholds. We demolish arguments and every pretension that sets

itself up against knowledge of God, and we take captive every thought to make it obedient to Christ. (2 Corinthians 10:4–5)

If Paul had been using the weapons of the world, he would have used a power maneuver to deal with his critics. But he realized the battle is not just against earthly critics. He had to deal with spiritual powers in the unseen world, so he used weapons that have divine power to demolish spiritual strongholds. These weapons include prayer and pleas for God's aid, as well as the intervention of heavenly warriors on God's side to battle the unseen spiritual forces behind the critics.

Many people who continue to struggle with self-blame are trapped in a spiritual stronghold. So rather than simply attack the flesh-and-blood problem, let's take guidance from Paul. Attack the spiritual stronghold. When it crumbles, the problem will erode away.

Believing that you will fail

We all fail at times. But if you struggle with self-condemnation, it's likely that you believe you are headed toward repeated failure. So, hoping that a lofty goal will motivate you to better behavior, you are prone to set unrealistic standards. But what that usually does is to set you up for even more failure. Your standards are so high that you will never measure up.

The roots of too-high standards, as we have seen, can lie in the past. But often the causes can be found in the present.

Reasons in the Present That We Set Our Standards Too High

Overly high standards are fueled by theological reasons, pride, a legal understanding of justice, and defensiveness. While it can be good to hold ourselves to a high standard—after all, who wants to be careless in the way they live and think—how strict should our standards be?

Theological influences

Self-blame is often a result of our perceived wrongdoing. But we each hold a different standard that defines what is wrong. For one person, a moment of sexual attraction toward someone not their spouse leads to serious guilt. For another person, momentary attraction is expected, but dwelling on sexual fantasies produces feelings of guilt. For yet another, no guilt is felt unless thoughts and fantasies lead to action. Personal standards and individual interpretations of biblical prohibitions, of course, affect when people believe they have crossed a line from good person to moral failure.

One's religion also can affect what we think of as wrong.[1]

In his sermon on the mount, Jesus said, "You have heard that it was said, 'Do not commit adultery.' But I tell you that anyone who looks at a woman lustfully has already committed adultery with her in his heart (Matthew 5:27–28). Did Jesus's teaching require an unblemished thought life, or was he encouraging his followers to rely on God, not themselves? Concerned about the temptations of hypocrisy and self-justification, Jesus championed the idea that our thought life really matters. When we understand that, it becomes much more difficult to believe we can lead righteous lives based on our own efforts. So we are led to trust God for help in righteous living.

No one believes that a lustful thought has the same social- and character-destructive effects as an illicit affair (even though they equally are indications of our need for God's redemption). But sometimes people can make themselves feel just as guilty over a fleeting sexual attraction as if they had carried on an affair.

A legal understanding of justice

Just as theological interpretations differ, legal understandings of justice also differ. In terms of violating human laws, there are *subjectivist* and *objectivist* stances toward crime.[2]

Subjectivists believe that if a person has a settled intent to commit a crime and takes a clear step (such as casing a house as plans are made to steal items from the home), then the crime is essentially committed and punishment is in order. Objectivists believe no-harm-no-foul: if a burglar is caught before carrying goods away, he or she is not guilty of theft, just breaking and entering. But there is a limit. Objectivists believe that what is known as "dangerous proximity" is equivalent to committing the crime. In dangerous proximity, a person very close to consummating an illegal act—perhaps walking out the door with a pocket full of jewelry (but not, technically speaking, having gotten completely outside) is considered to have done the act.

The point is this: Standards and definitions vary, and expectations for the appropriate punishment of wrongdoing vary just as much. We each tend to think that our standards are rightly calibrated, and we assume that our view is shared by others. But we can't be certain that our standards are accurate when compared to an absolute, authoritative standard.

Pride

Pride is an issue for all of us, and perhaps we are so puffed up that we really do think we should be perfect. Having that expectation, we are convinced that we should never fail to meet the standard. Pride can lead to setting standards too high. The underlying message is "I can defeat human limitations." I realized this in myself. I was similar to C. S. Lewis's fictional character Reepicheep[3]—the comic yet sympathetic Narnian mouse—looking for a chance to use my skill and effort to overcome all imperfections.

More often than not, pride lies at the root of standards that are too high and expectations that are too grand. Our battle against unrealistic standards needs to take its cues not from a sword-wielding, bravado-filled mouse (like we often are), but from Jesus, the Conqueror. We cannot break free without God's help.

Psychological defensiveness

On the other hand, we might set our standards too high as a psychological defense against failure. Some people are terrified of failing. Sometimes they reason (often subconsciously), *If I set my standards so high that* no one *could succeed, then I can't blame myself for failing.* They might hold on to admittedly unrealistic standards as a protection against failing to measure up to the majority of humans. As long as they can blame the obvious—"I expect way too much of myself. What can I say?"—they don't have to face the less obvious reality, which is that they actually did cause harm to someone.

HOLDING HIGH STANDARDS

I am not advocating relaxed standards of thought, behavior, or morality. We should try to live to the highest standards—always following the example of Jesus's life. We might call those *hoped-for standards.* Those are the behaviors we would practice if the image of God within us were free to manifest itself at all times without contamination. Unfortunately, our inner life is contaminated by sin.

Having a fallen nature does not let us off the hook morally, of course. God holds us responsible; he will judge our works (see Revelation 20:12; Psalm 62:12; Romans 2:6; 1 Peter 1:17). But God will exercise a different judgment on Christians (see James 3:1). While our impure works may be consumed, we will be saved if we are followers of Jesus (see 1 Corinthians 3:15).

God will judge our works and our hearts. And that is the point we should hold on to. We are not appointed to be the judge of others or ourselves (see Matthew 7:1–6), but we must discern rightly, fairly, and nondefensively the personal and social consequences of our sins. We have to do that first, before we try to right the wrongs that we can seek to rectify.

As I worked through Step 3—Rethink Ruminations—I realized I was judging myself by unrealistic benchmarks. After conducting a careful self-analysis, I had an idea of what my problems were and what I thought God wanted to do in me to enable me to deal with the unrealistic expectations.

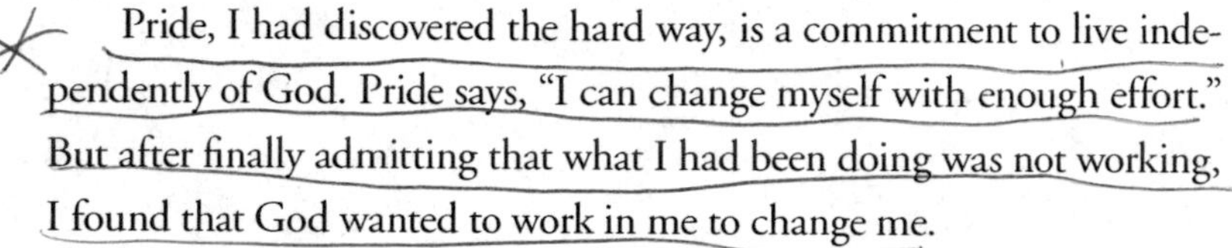

Pride, I had discovered the hard way, is a commitment to live independently of God. Pride says, "I can change myself with enough effort." But after finally admitting that what I had been doing was not working, I found that God wanted to work in me to change me.

Uprooting Your Unrealistic Expectations

Each of us needs to pull unrealistic expectations and standards up by the roots. I identified the sources of my problems as Satan, sin, and self.

Dealing with Satan

We are told in James 4:7–8 and 1 Peter 5:8–9 to draw near to God and resist the devil and then the devil will flee from us. Satan is no match for God's power and protection (see Ephesians 6:10–18). God stands behind us and in front of us, and God lives within us. Jesus, living in us through his Spirit, puts the devil to flight. So to uproot problem expectations, I must draw near to God, resist the devil, and trust that a real Champion will defend me.

When I am confronted with accusations or lies from Satan, such as the deception that I am not forgiven, I can defeat the accusations by telling myself God's truth—that God forgives those who confess their sins to him. That is another way to avoid getting sucked once again into the wrath of self-condemnation.

Dealing with sin

In Romans 6:16, we are told that we choose who will be master over us. Will sin have the upper hand, or will we agree to unite ourselves to Jesus? Paul admonishes us to defeat sin in our lives by joining Jesus. Whichever we choose, our focus will be to serve the chosen master. Using this understanding, sin is dealt with by fixing my attention on what the Master wants and by bonding myself to the Master's will. In that way, I don't have to stand up against sin myself and defeat it alone. And thus, I need not try to measure up to my own standards of perfectionism.

Dealing with self

In Romans 7:14–25, Paul wrestled with his weakness, stating that he was powerless, on his own, to achieve self-control. While we have a responsibility to control our words and behavior, we can't fight off sin on our own. At the end of this passage on self-control, Paul came to a realization. He asked, "Who will rescue me from this body of death?" (verse 24). And his answer, of course, was and is Jesus. So whether we are dealing with Satan, sin, or self, there is one answer that is at the root of healing—to connect with Jesus. True healing will happen only to the degree to which we are able to make and maintain an intimate, ongoing connection with Jesus.

Our part in exerting self-control, however, is not trivial. We can employ some of the methods developed by psychology and by Christians through the years. The spiritual disciplines can help greatly. (See, for example, Richard Foster and Gayle Beebe, *Longing for God: Seven Paths of*

Christian Devotion.)[4] Meditations and particular types of prayer—such as the Jesus Prayer or the *lectio divina*—have been used with dramatic results.

Psychology can provide additional aids to self-control.[5] These include changing behaviors and practices that are closely related to spiritual goals. Psychology also can help create a space where Jesus can work more easily because now we are cooperating. This is an example of Ephesians 2:8–10 and Philippians 2:12, where we are to trust God and to work out our own salvation, both. Some of the cognitive behavioral counseling methods help with controlling rumination. Rumination can be controlled to a degree by stopping negative thinking, as we will see in the following chapter. When we slip into that old pattern, we catch ourselves and replace negative rumination with more productive thinking. We might direct ourselves to pray, or to engage in a different activity.

For example, Kirby plays CDs of Christian music to keep her mind focused. Or take a simple step, such as changing locations. For instance, if I am at my desk, I might leave the room to get a cup of coffee. It helps to interrupt your ruminating by making a deliberate change—even a simple one.

Other methods include planning a strategy ahead of time to avoid situations where you are likely to ruminate. For example, it is more likely that you will fall into rumination if you are alone. So if you know in advance that you will be by yourself for an afternoon, evening, or weekend, plan to invest your time and energies in something useful.

Having identified the sources of my perfectionism and workaholism, I developed a plan to replace unrealistic expectations with healthier choices. First, I would rely more on Jesus. Second, I would employ time-honored methods developed by Christians over the centuries. I increased my devotional time to at least one hour out of the two that I set aside in the mornings, and I often went beyond that. I was rereading books by some of my favorite authors, including Oswald Chambers, Malcolm Muggeridge, Richard Foster, Max Lucado, Andrew Murray, and C. S. Lewis. Third, I wanted to employ some of the methods of psychology to help deal with negating unrealistic standards and expectations.

Although I had a plan, I had not yet broken free. That was not going to happen until later, during the summer. And it was going to take a crisis plus some time of reflection—as well as a lot of hard work—to take me through the next step to self-forgiveness.

14

Run Rumination Out of Town

Decide now that you will tell yourself no more lies

> Do not be too timid and squeamish about your actions. All life is an experiment. The more experiments you make the better. What if they are a little coarse and you may get your coat soiled or torn? What if you do fail, and get fairly rolled in the dirt once or twice? Up again, and you shall never be so afraid of a tumble.
>
> —Ralph Waldo Emerson

Rumination is not a word that comes up often in everyday conversation. In this discussion, rumination refers to obsessively dwelling on negative thoughts and images. This isn't good for us.

Rumination is the universal bad boy of mental health. It has been associated with most of the leading mental-health disorders. It is highly involved with posttraumatic stress disorder, but also plays a major role in depression, anxiety, generalized anxiety disorder, panic disorder, obsessive-compulsive disorders, obsessive-compulsive anxiety disorders, and anger disorders. It also is a factor in psychological disorders that affect physical health, such as psychosomatic disorders or physical disorders associated with worry and rumination, such as colitis or heart palpitations. In short, if you get the chance to ruminate, don't. If you get the chance to stop ruminating, do.

As a university professor, I probably live a more thought-centered life than most people. It's what professors do all day—think. (Or at least that's what we are supposed to do.) Prior to my brother's suicide, I was not prone to pondering the past. But after Mike ended his life, I couldn't control my rumination. Even as Kirby and I traveled across Europe, I kept rethinking my mother's murder and my brother's subsequent suicide. The puddles of blood in my mother's hallway, my brother slumped over his desk, limp hand extended across a letter addressed to me. It didn't end. I reexperienced my feelings and failings as a brother again and again. This lasted years.

I didn't feel depressed or angry or anxious. I just felt unsettled. It never got so bad that it disrupted my life, but the feeling was always there. It led to frequent long periods of brooding.

When Paul had his thorn in the flesh (see 2 Corinthians 12:7), God comforted him with the truth that God's grace was sufficient. I had often experienced the sufficiency of God's grace. But this time, it seemed only to be a topical anesthetic spray that temporarily calmed the immediate itching and did not extract the thorn.

The Science of Rumination

My colleague Jack Berry, several other colleagues, and I studied rumination in 2004.[1] Jack came to work with me in 1997 as a postdoctoral researcher, when I had a grant to study forgiveness. Jack thrived on doing statistics. He spent hours trying this analysis and that analysis, until at last the data gave up their secrets.

In 2000 Jack and I were developing a measure of trait forgivingness, which might seem to be worded awkwardly, but it is the way psychologists talk about a tendency to forgive lots of situations and maintain that trait for years. Jack and I began looking at what kept people from forgiving others, and rumination was center stage. We found, among other things, that what people ruminate about accounts for what they feel. The effect on their emotions then can prevent or, at the very least, make it hard for them to forgive others.

When Kirby and I were in Europe, in the months following Mike's suicide, I realized I could use this scientific knowledge. It mattered what my ruminations were because they would lead directly to my feelings. I was concerned about Charlene and David and their loss of a husband and father. I knew that my empathy for them was a good thing, and that empathy made me want to help them. But I also had darker thoughts—self-centered thoughts. If I could separate those tangled emotions, that might give me a clue as to how to handle the negative rumination and still be empathic to those who were suffering.

Guilt topped the list of where my negative ruminations took me. I was keenly aware that I had failed my brother, and I was ashamed of the failures. I felt sorrow, frustration, and regret over my failures. Usually, I would do something about problems rather than stew about them. But, being in Europe and traveling, I could not follow any of my typical courses of action. So add frustration to the guilt, and toss in shame, regret, remorse, and grief.

Rumination can drag you into the quicksand of despair. And you can easily get lost in self-pity. But while we can get ourselves into trouble through making unwise and immoral decisions, not every bit of suffering is brought on by our poor moral choices. Sometimes problems just happen. And we often can't, on our own, haul ourselves out of the pit of despair. It is only by looking up and extending our hands and our eyes to God that we can see the way out.

Thus, as Kirby and I trekked about Europe, while we stayed at

Cambridge, and even back home in Virginia, I indulged my self-pity and frustration while fighting to stay out of the quicksand. I knew that inspir-

ing self-pity was a trick of Satan's to pull me away from the Lord. I knew that I needed to resist the devil so he would flee (see James 4:7). I knew that the Lord is my help (see Psalms 33:20; 46:1; 118:14). Yet I couldn't resolve my negative feelings. And that made me feel even more frustrated and guilty. Guilt piled upon guilt.

With the clarity of hindsight, I can see that in part I was trying to

punish myself. And I was doing a good job of it. I was miserable. I needed something to break me out of the same-old same-old.

Deciding to Defeat Negative Thinking

Facing self-condemnation head-on requires that you take charge of your thoughts. Self-condemnation usually is characterized by negative, self-judging thoughts that tie into a single theme and gang up on you. The danger comes in rumination.

There is one way in which worry can be a good thing. It helps us analyze situations and plan responses. When we are facing a dangerous or important task, worry focuses our mind to help us explore different solutions. When the work of worrying is at its best, it gives our thinking greater focus to help us solve problems. If worry causes you to ask the right questions and follow them through to the most likely outcome, you can anticipate whether the action will be constructive or not. It is only

when worry crosses over into rumination that it becomes a negative force.

How Rumination Works

Rumination is worry run amok. It focuses your attention on emotions that are intended to help you survive a threat. But rumination gets bogged down into repetitive, emotion-based questioning. Remember, effective worry is about asking different questions and following the reasoning to its logical conclusion. Rumination asks questions, tosses up doubts, and asks the same questions or new ones based on catastrophic fear. It never gets around to generating solutions and evaluating which ones place us on the best course for constructive action. Rumination tends to be organized around negative emotions, and it loops unendingly in a cycle of fear, sadness, anger, frustration, or helplessness.

How rumination feeds self-condemnation

Part of the human condition is to give ourselves a lot of credit. This is called the self-enhancing bias. For example, if a husband and wife are asked individually what percentage of that person's effort is typically invested in the marriage, the two estimates added together almost always total more than one hundred percent. The practical result of the self-enhancing bias is that we almost always believe we can solve the problems that life deals us—and solve them well. The bias feeds our unrealistic expectations and perfectionistic standards.

Any failure to solve a problem leads quickly to rumination. It can render you immobile or trap you in a rut. This is a double-edged sword. Not only can you not solve the problems, but you are failing to measure up to your own expectation that you should have solved the problems long ago. You are now doubly condemned.

If we add social pressures, things get worse. Suppose a well-meaning friend asks, "Why can't you kick this self-blame? Snap out of it." The friend has just added another dimension—social disappointment. Triply condemned!

Each level ratchets up the pressure, making failure more severe and more discouraging and crushing you deeper into the mire. But the good news is there are solutions.

CONQUERING RUMINATION

The following solutions have been developed and perfected with people whose struggle with self-blame had pushed them into clinical levels of depression, anxiety, anger, and stress. Here is the quick version of what the psychotherapies recommend. If you are beset with chronic rumination and you cannot get substantial relief from what I advise in this chapter, you might consult some of the self-help resources mentioned in a footnote below* or seek the help of a friend or counselor.

Understand the nature of troublesome thinking

The first step toward undoing rumination is to understand the type of thinking that causes problems. Several types of thinking fall into this category, including faulty beliefs and assumptions (extending to expectations and cognitive processes) and unhelpful thoughts and mental images.

Faulty beliefs and assumptions. Faulty beliefs carry a hidden threat in that we wrongly view them as being helpful. These might be slightly paranoid worries that life is unfair, our boss is prejudiced against us, or no one understands us. We accept the validity of these assumptions and believe we need to guard against the forces that oppose us. Interestingly, everyday life reinforces such faulty beliefs.

In the brilliant movie *The Dream Team,*[2] four recovering schizophrenic patients, who have made remarkable progress at dealing with their mental illnesses, are set adrift in New York City. Their psychiatrist

---

*Take advantage of these resources:

Aaron T. Beck, John Rush, Brian F. Shaw, and Gary Emery, *Cognitive Therapy of Depression* (New York: Guilford Press, 1979).

Joyce Meyer, *Me and My Big Mouth: Your Answer Is Right Under Your Nose* (New York: Warner Books, 2002).

Chris Thurman, *The Lies We Believe* (Nashville: Thomas Nelson, 1999).

witnesses a murder but is hit in the head and hospitalized, leaving the patients to solve the murder and save the psychiatrist from being murdered too. (Don't you just hate it when that happens?)

In one of my favorite scenes, two who suffer from paranoid schizophrenia, characterized by a false belief system, are on the top floor of a building. They want to get out of the building quickly. One, who also has a problem with explosive anger, presses the button to summon an elevator. The elevator takes a few seconds and—confirmed in his belief that nothing happens without intimidation—he unleashes his anger on the elevator button by pounding it and then kicking the elevator door.

A second patient, who believes he is Jesus, extends one finger dramatically and touches the button. The light above the elevator dings and the door opens. Both patients have had their expectations confirmed. Life circumstances reinforced their faulty assumptions. On a less-dramatic level, life also reinforces our faulty assumptions, which makes it harder for us to identify them and address them effectively.

Faulty expectations. Closely linked to faulty beliefs and assumptions are faulty expectations. Expectations describe how people think the future will unfold. For instance, we may expect that all problems will quickly go away or that bad moods won't last. When our faulty expectations are not met we get disappointed. We can blame ourselves for the failure, even when it isn't our fault. And in doing so, we increase self-blame.

Faulty cognitive processes. Ruminations call forth faulty patterns of thinking. Here are several examples that follow the internal monologue of a fictitious woman, Suzette, who is plagued by self-condemnation. Suzette feels she has failed in caring for her aging mother, who recently was diagnosed with Alzheimer's disease. Here are Suzette's struggles, described by type.

Dichotomous reasoning is seeing things in all-or-nothing terms. ("Mom didn't complain when she raised me, and I shouldn't complain now that I'm the parent.")

Overgeneralization is going well beyond the facts to hypothesize outcomes that are not supported by logic or the established facts. ("I've been stretched to the limit, and I can't take it if it gets worse, which it almost certainly will.")

Jumping to conclusions occurs when people take a reasonable premise but jump far beyond the outcome that can reasonably be anticipated to reach an extremely negative conclusion. ("Probably she will have a rapid decline. Or worse, what if she doesn't? I'll be caregiving forever.")

Exaggeration refers to making things seem worse than they are. Often these are expressed in absolute statements, such as Suzette characterizing the situation with "I never," "people always," or "no one cares." When one says "never," "always," or "no one," those are exaggerations. There is almost nothing in the world that always or never occurs.

Catastrophizing is exaggeration cranked up a notch until it has become something unbearable. ("If I put my mom in a care facility, her life savings will soon be eaten up, and she'll be destitute. Then, keeping her in the home will bankrupt my family.")

Questioning the known is doubting a statement of fact, which elevates the uncertainty. ("Sure, the doctor says Mom will eventually get worse, but it will happen very slowly. But I know he's just putting a good face on it.")

Stuck in a rut is to repeat the same line of reasoning incessantly. ("I'm such a bad daughter, I'm such a bad daughter, I'm such a bad daughter.")

Discounting progress is admitting that some progress has been made, but then saying that the progress isn't important. ("I try and try to control my temper. Sure, once in a while I can do so, but that's usually when I've had a good day.") Using words such as *should* and *ought* usually are self-condemning. They blame the self for not meeting some standard—often an unreachable or seldom reachable standard. ("I should be able to figure this out myself.")

Unreasoning self-condemnation occurs when Suzette feels it's appropriate to condemn herself for something she had no control over. ("I have cared for my mother for three years now, and it's obvious that she keeps declining. My failure to help her proves that I'm a terrible daughter.")

ACT NOW TO OVERCOME RUMINATION

The first step to running rumination out of town is to recognize the types of thinking that typically cause you problems. Doing this will initially heighten your awareness of the problem, which can make you feel discouraged. Fortunately, cognitive psychotherapists have developed ways to deal with these troublesome thoughts. First, you must understand the idea behind cognitive therapies. Second, apply specific methods to help yourself think more positively. Third, focus on maintaining the positive changes.

Cognitive therapy addresses the mistaken idea that people and events, as well as the words and reactions of others, cause a person to be angry, afraid, or sad. The truth is, our own thoughts—rather than external events and circumstances—cause those emotions. Suppose Joe's boss yells at him for being late with a project. Because Joe is angry with his boss, he spits in his boss's coffee. (Yes, Joe probably was toilet trained too early.) Joe's excuse for his inexcusable behavior is simple: "He made me mad."

But Joe's boss yelling at him did not really make him angry. Joe's boss yells at most of the workers, but only Joe spat in the man's coffee. Other employees react differently. LaShonda gets depressed. Bjorn gets anxious. Why the contrasting reactions? Because each person thinks different things. Joe thinks, *Who does my boss think he is? He has no right to disrespect me. I'll teach him a thing or two.* LaShonda thinks, *Oh, dear, he hates me. I'm a worthless employee. The company would be better off if I were to find a different job.* Bjorn thinks, *Shoot, I've done it again. This is probably the last time the boss is going to put up with my mistakes.* Being yelled at is not what determines their emotions or their reactions. It is their thoughts about having been yelled at that affect them.

Change your thinking

If your thinking determines your emotions and behaviors, you need to pay close attention to your thinking. By becoming aware of what you think, you can target the thinking that brings forth emotions and behaviors you want to change. And the good news is that you *can* change those ways of thinking. Here's how.

Recognize your repeated patterns and make a commitment to change the patterns. Patterns of thinking, not one-off thoughts, are what you need to pay attention to. By getting at the patterns you most often employ, you can make the best strategic investment in trying to change.

Learn to interrupt the flow. God designed our minds to be efficient. Once we get moving down a mental track, it is like getting a train moving. Once it picks up speed it's hard to switch it to a different track. Instead, it will remain on the same track and will reach its logical endpoint. Committing yourself to think differently (and writing it down), and then becoming aware of your patterns, will put you in position to disrupt the patterns. But you also can take other actions to derail troublesome thoughts. You can build switches into the track to shunt negative thinking onto tracks that will take you to more positive destinations. When you detect a problematic thought pattern, imagine that an alarm sounds. Stop immediately. Think something more productive by substituting a different pattern for the one you want to end.

3. *Be aware of what won't help.* Paradoxically, it will not help you to think, *Stop! Don't go there.* Studies show that thought suppression—trying to stop a train of thoughts with nothing to take its place—doesn't work. Harvard psychologist Daniel Wegner told people to try not to think of white bears, but if the thought of such a bear intruded, to ring a bell. The harder the person tried not to think about white bears, the more he or she pounded the bell.[3]

So don't bother instructing yourself that you should not believe a certain way. Don't say to yourself, *I should not expect negative events. Don't ruminate. Don't imagine myself failing.* (I hope you appreciate the irony of my telling you what not to do.)

So how do you stop? Use a method that was used by many of the subjects in Wegner's studies. "How did you try not to think about white bears?" the experimenter would ask.

"I thought about black bears."

Aha! Deliberately think about something else. Sometimes the simplest and most effective way to interrupt the flow is through distraction. Another winning strategy is to change your usual activities. We get into patterns of behaviors, and those behaviors can fix our way of thinking. Change your activities and you'll find it's easier to change your thinking. One final way to root out rumination is to find a new frame for your image of yourself and the relationships you live in.

Here's a real-life example. One woman was overwhelmed with her responsibilities and her pattern of thinking of herself as a failure of a mother. But she changed her life by becoming aware of the challenges she was successfully and courageously dealing with. Her courage became the new frame for her image of herself. With that change, her few failures faded to the background.

Cognitive therapy is about reframing—seeing things in a new perspective. By analyzing thoughts and images, people can replace problematic thoughts and images with those that are more realistic and less troublesome and problematic. But it isn't enough just to gain such useful insights. You must make the changes in your daily life, which is difficult. Learning to defeat self-condemning rumination is like learning to be better at a sport or learning to use a new computer application. It requires understanding, systematic practice of specific steps, and the will to get back into the game after trying and failing.

- Decide you will try to improve. Improvement develops much more quickly when you intentionally aim to improve. Find the motivation that will get you moving. Ask yourself what you would like to be different—specifically. Write down your concrete goal. If you know where you hope to go, you'll be more likely to get there.
- Practice. To improve, you must consciously seek to do as well as you can, again and again. Vince Lombardi, former coach of the Green Bay Packers, was fond of saying, "Practice doesn't make perfect. Perfect practice makes perfect." While we don't want to derail ourselves back into the trap of perfectionism, Lombardi's point is vital. Practice hard. Don't just run through the motions.
- Set definite goals. Pick one or two small changes to work on. We can't remake our mental life all at once. So take it a step or two at a time. Learn basic skills, such as the cognitive skills covered in this chapter. Also, set goals that fit the realities of your everyday living. Think about situations you often face. What will you do differently in those situations? The changes you make in your thoughts as you reflect on goals and your life must be put into action.
- Monitor your progress. Progress comes slowly and often in fits and starts. You need to monitor your progress often

enough that you can use it as a motivator for additional progress. But because most progress comes slowly, don't monitor it so frequently that you'll become discouraged by day after day of seeing no progress or only microscopic improvement. It might be a good idea to take stock on Sunday afternoon each week. If you schedule a time for self-evaluation into your routine, you'll be more likely to do it.

- Set new standards. As you achieve your goals, set new ones. But don't forget to keep practicing the previous goals. Any time you try to make a change in an established negative habit, you'll usually be critical about your failure to turn it around immediately. But tell yourself, *So what! If I fail, no harm. If I succeed, even just a little, I'm better off!* Defeat the fears that try to stop you from changing. 
- Get back on the horse. A rider who is bucked off must get back on the horse. Courage is acting well in spite of fear and setbacks.

Once you are on the road to controlling self-condemning ruminations, you can aim at making important social changes. Those are necessary if you are to reach the point where you can responsibly forgive yourself and experience emotional forgiveness as part of that step. To help you get there, remember that it's essential to work on making things right with others.

CHANGING STANDARDS AND EXPECTATIONS

As we have seen, we can change our behavior. We can reframe the standards we impose on ourselves. And we can shift our reliance away from ourselves and toward God to help us change. Change requires your total reliance on Jesus to defeat your three biggest opponents: Satan, sin, and the power of self. Arm yourself as well with time-tested methods such as prayer, confession, meditation, and reliance on others.

In my own odyssey, I had received forgiveness from God, and I was able to make amends directly by honoring Mike's request to straighten out the family finances. I made amends indirectly through my research and speaking. God had gotten our derailed relationship back on track, and I had drawn on both Christian and psychological methods to rein in my perfectionism and workaholism. Things were looking up, though I felt progress was fragile and change was incomplete.

I still had not experienced emotional self-forgiveness and self-acceptance. And worse, a major and unexpected test loomed on the horizon.

Part 6

Step 4:
REACH Emotional Self-Forgiveness

15

Standing the Test

Your hard-won gains will face major challenges

> To forgive is to set a prisoner free and discover that the prisoner was you.
>
> —Lewis B. Smedes

The test came in late March 2008. The doctoral program in counseling psychology at Virginia Commonwealth University was rocked to its core when one of our leading students committed suicide.

Any suicide is hard for a community of people who love the lost person. But those in our doctoral program were particularly close. And as counseling psychologists, we have devoted our lives to helping people deal with emotional problems that might otherwise lead them to suicide. Those in the counseling psychology program faced the same struggles that I faced when my brother had committed suicide. We not only felt personal loss but also deep professional failure. *Why couldn't we see it coming? Why couldn't we help her?* we kept asking ourselves.

Of course, we knew that Jane (as I'll call her) had been struggling, and some of her close friends at church and in the program had been talking to her. Jane was a dark-haired young woman with a pleasant, open face. She was from China. She told me that she had taken a master's degree in medical research, but her Christian values had redirected her toward counseling, where she could help people directly. She was an excellent counselor, but we knew she missed her family and friends in China.

The week before she killed herself, she came to see me about an administrative task. I knew she had been struggling emotionally. So, after we dealt with the paperwork, I asked, "How are you doing?"

She teared up. "I'm sad. I often think that if I could get back home, I'd be okay."

"You miss your family."

"Terribly. When I counsel, I listen to people describe their problems. It makes me think of home even more. US students don't have as much... *connection*...with family as we do in China." She took a tissue from the box on my table.

"It sounds like working at your counseling placement might not be best for you right now, Jane."

"It will be fine. I'll get through this month. Then maybe I'll go home."

"You seem under a lot of stress. Do you have enough support to handle it?"

"It's nice of you to ask, Ev. I have my church, and some support from others here in the counseling program. I'm okay. I cry a lot. But I can handle it. I'll get through this." She gathered her papers. "I'd better run. I have to go back to my counseling practicum. Thank you for caring about me."

"Take care of yourself, Jane."

"I will."

A week later, she was dead. Her depression had been too much for her.

I was personally devastated. For a day or two it seemed like a slow-motion replay of Mike's suicide. It was a test. I've heard someone say,

"God gives the test first, and then the lesson." I had learned many lessons in dealing with Mike's death. Now the test was whether I could use them.

The aftermath of Jane's suicide flipped me back to running on the streets in the north of Paris. Mind whirling in the fog of emotions, I again climbed the steps up Montmartre to Sacré Coeur. I recalled the shame of being unable to help.

In contrast, I remembered, too, what I had found at the top—the assurance that I was not alone in suffering, that Jesus was at my side and understood pain. My mind flitted to standing on the platform at the Chautauqua Institution and saying, "I don't understand fully what happened, and I don't know whether I will ever be able to fully understand it, but I know this happened for a purpose, and perhaps one day I'll be able to help others deal with such things." I flashed back to the little English garden in Cambridge where I had worked through my thinking on suicide. I recalled the gratitude of being able to help straighten out the family finances Mike had left in disarray. Now, with those in our program who were devastated by Jane's suicide, I knew that God had prepared me to help. But would I again be triggered by painful shame?

The counseling program scheduled a memorial meeting. At home, at five o'clock that morning in March, I prayed for clarity and direction on what I might say at the meeting. Then I began to write in my journal.

That afternoon we gathered in the dissertation room—a beautiful room that is on the walking tour of historic sites in Richmond. It was packed. The room seemed darker than usual, as if a light had gone out. Many of us shared memories of Jane. We tried, through telling anecdotes, to re-create for others our experiences with Jane so we could create a lasting common memory of what she had meant to us individually and to our community. We were all feeling guilty over not having done enough to help. Near the end of the meeting, I opened my journal and began to read aloud:

Jane, our friend, has passed from us. Our hearts go out to her family. Our hearts are saddened and deeply grieved by her loss from our community.

Only the week before she died, Jane sat in my office. I could see her depression, yet I could not reach out to prevent her death. This has happened to me before. Bound, chained, restrained, unable to help. There is always a lot of guilt—too much—to go around in times like these. We think things like *Couldn't I have done more?* Silence breathes back in our ear. Yet we can't become absorbed in our guilt, our anger, our self-recrimination, our self-condemnation, our sadness, our loss.

Instead, we must remember Jane and her positive impact on our community. The love she had for us has touched us. We are transformed. Even the bitterness of death cannot undo that love.

Yet, we admit that our emotions are so mixed. We are angry at depression and death. We are saddened at our loss and feel empathy, sympathy, compassion, and love for her family, her clients, and ourselves, her friends. We are sad in losing the love we lost at Jane's passing. It hurts so much that a young, vibrant woman who was full of life and promise should be taken, what seems to us, before her time. We each will remember Jane, I am sure, for the rest of our lives. We don't know why things like this happen. I believe that no matter how long I live, I'll be confused and upset by death, particularly suicide. It is an evil enemy that has struck my heart twice now. I know it is too early for us to process this thought, but I want to say it because it was eventually meaningful to me when I lost my brother to suicide. The thought is this: Even if I do not know

> why, I know that I personally am called to try, within the turmoil of my own emotions, to help others during their times of turmoil. I am inadequate in the face of death, yet as a counselor, I know I will be called, throughout my life, to help others who experience loss and pain to the fullest. Yet to step back in later times once the emotions have subsided and to learn how we can help others better. But that is for later.
>
> As for now, we offer a tribute to this young Christian woman, who was so full of life and love and who graced our lives. Jane, we will miss you most terribly.

A TIME OF REFLECTION

In early August that year, I went to Florida to finish a half-written book, *A Just Forgiveness.*[1] My brother-in-law Wayne owns a condominium in Jupiter, Florida, and he graciously allows me to use it a month each summer as a writing retreat. I can concentrate on my work there, without the distractions of meetings, e-mail, phone calls, or conversation—except talking daily to Kirby by phone. Going there was a perfect chance to get close to God again.

Even though I was writing about forgiveness, it was *self*-forgiveness that was more readily on my mind. Jane's suicide had reawakened many of the tumultuous emotions I had been working through. I felt that her death—while an important loss for me and for our community—had been a personal test for me. At Chautauqua Institution in 2005, I had expressed faith that someday I would be able to draw on my experience of Mike's death to help others. Then Jane's death had tossed me, again, into the emotional whirlpool. But this time I was not sucked under. Even in my raw emotions in the days after her death, I had been able to provide some help to others. In Florida, four months after Jane's death, I could see—by looking back at that test—how much God had healed me.

I had not frozen and defended myself through inaction. I had not decided to flee—to leave the situation, lose myself in work, or not engage emotionally—as I might have done in the past. And I had not fought against the pain, angry at the death as I had been when I lost Mike. Instead, I stayed engaged, let myself experience deep loss and hurt, let myself grieve. But I also did not let myself hide within those emotions. I tried to be available to others to ease their burdens.

I remember an anecdote about a successful businessman. Asked to explain the secret to his success, he said, "Two words: 'good decisions.'"

"How did you learn to make good decisions?" he was asked.

"Two words," he said, "'bad decisions.'"

I had, like that man, learned through mistakes. The initial test was Mike's suicide. God taught me the needed lessons from my failures. Then, in God's mercy, there came another test. That time I was able to rely more on God and to focus on others. I passed the test.

But in Florida, I realized I had still not fully forgiven myself for my failings in Mike's death. I had made things right with God and the others affected, and I had decided to forgive myself. But I had never allowed myself to deal with my deepest emotions. I needed *emotional* self-forgiveness. In 2003, I had written about emotional forgiveness in *Forgiving and Reconciling: Bridges to Wholeness and Hope.*[2] But I had never worked through the steps to forgiveness that are captured in the acronym REACH to arrive at emotional self-forgiveness. Now seemed to be the time.

16

Take Five Steps to REACH Emotional Self-Forgiveness

What it takes to move forward from saying it to feeling it

> I don't know if I continue, even today, always liking myself. But what I learned to do many years ago was to forgive myself.
>
> —Maya Angelou

The REACH Forgiveness method has helped many people who tried to forgive others but kept struggling with it. The method began as a way to help spouses who were in counseling to forgive their partners. We found that it also worked well in small groups and has been used effectively in churches around the world, in schools, and in a variety of counseling settings. (Go to www.people.vcu.edu/~eworth/ for free downloadable Word files for manuals to help leaders and participants in both Christian and secular groups.)

I was the originator of the REACH Forgiveness approach,[1] which has been tested and verified all over the world. But when I found myself continuing to struggle with emotional self-forgiveness, would I be able to systematically work through the five steps? And would this approach, which has worked for so many others, work for me? I put it to the test.

REACH EMOTIONAL SELF-FORGIVENESS

The acronym REACH is designed to help people easily remember the five steps. Here they are in order.

R = Recall My Hurtful Acts

The first step involves recalling the hurt. I remembered times I had hurt Mike. I tried to recall what it was like hearing about Mike's death and the period afterward. I thought through my months spent in Cambridge. I also recalled the day I made the decision to forgive myself. I spent the first day on this step.

E = Emotionally Replace Unforgiveness with Empathy Toward the One Who Hurt Me (i.e., Myself)

At the outset of the second morning, I focused on empathizing with Mike. What must he have felt that was so painful that it drove him to kill himself? I considered his life, his job, his interactions with his son and his wife, whom he loved. The more I empathized with Mike, the more I realized that I was not a central character in his despair. I realized at an emotional level—not just head knowledge—that my failures had not driven Mike to suicide. This was not making excuses for my failures or justifying myself. I had already faced the hard truth that I had let him down. But empathy brought with it a cooling mercy toward my guilt.

Then I tried to empathize with myself. I relived the tense conversation between Mike and me at the Chinese restaurant, as well as my childish "whatever!" when Mike refused to take my advice to see a counselor. I regularly give clients the benefit of the doubt, affirm their worth when they are overwhelmed by family patterns of interacting, and affirm that they are not perfect and don't have to be. But I couldn't usually give that same mercy to myself. This time though, working through the steps of REACH, things were different.

I also empathized with myself for not meeting my own expectations. Yes, I wasn't perfect. Reacting to my past was natural. God expected me neither to be completely free of the past nor perfect in the present. Rather, God expected me to come to the divine throne with my imperfections and receive the covering that is afforded by Jesus's love.

Ironically, that realization renewed my self-blame—this time over how long it had taken me to come before God. I had hardened myself and coasted further from God, becoming cold in my anger. But I had confessed that. I knew God would forgive me. I empathized with my struggles to put into effect that which my brain knew and my heart too often seemed to muddy up.

The *E* step of REACH goes beyond simple empathy. The idea is to emotionally replace negative, unforgiving emotions with more positive emotions, such as sympathy, compassion, and love for yourself. It is useful to consider the parallels between forgiveness and self-forgiveness. When you forgive someone else, you acknowledge the wrong they did to you. Likewise, to forgive yourself you must acknowledge the wrong you did to someone, which caused them hurt and which has caused you regret. But it is counterproductive to beat yourself up because you have done wrong.

For me, empathy involved clearly admitting that I did wrong and understanding the reasons and the emotional factors that might have led to my wrongdoing. As I empathized, I felt myself changing, becoming more understanding of my mistakes. I didn't excuse them. I wanted to change. But I eased up on the stranglehold I had maintained around my own neck. I began to trust God to change me.

A = Altruistic Gift of Self-Forgiveness

The third day, I again practiced empathy. Then I tried to give myself an altruistic gift of forgiveness. That forgiveness was not just decisional forgiveness; that decision was made long ago. Today's task was not just about helping myself feel better; rather it was a gift of grace born from gratitude because I had been forgiven by God and by other people. Therefore I should try to give myself the same grace I would offer to someone else. I could recall things that Mike had done to provoke me and yet could forgive Mike for his failings. I tried to extend to myself the same gift of mercy in self-forgiveness. I felt the burdens finally lift.

C= Commit to the Emotional Self-Forgiveness That I Experienced

The fourth part of the model to REACH emotional forgiveness is to commit to the forgiveness I experienced. Often this can be enhanced through some type of ceremony or ritual. Early in the morning of the fourth day, I headed to Jupiter Beach to begin solidifying a new beginning.

Only the early risers were beaching it at 6:30 a.m. The tide was coming in. It was relaxing and gentle, but insistent. I found a big piece of coral on the beach—literally stubbing my toe on it. I piled a mound of sand around the coral, and I topped it with shells. The coral represented my heart. I thought of the shells atop the coral as a visible metaphor for God's love piercing through the pain to my heart. The sand represented the mound of self-blame and shame that kept the shells from touching my heart. I hoped that sand would be washed away by the waves of the Holy Spirit.

As the waves came in, they crept close to my sculpture. Finally, they broke on the sand. I could see the sand being leveled out. The tide came in with waves in sets, rather than at a steadily increasing pace. That reminded me of how my self-forgiveness experience had been—in starts and stops. Within ten minutes, the mound representing emotional self-condemnation had flattened out. It was being eroded as the waters lapped it. As the sand was washed away, shells kept shifting downward.

After thirty minutes there was just a ring of spread-out shells, with one resting atop the coral and the others all around it. To me this represented all the emotional self-blame being swept away. The beautiful shells scattered about represented the lessons God's love had taught me. Where self-blame had rested earlier, the waves—the Holy Spirit—could now touch my heart directly and surround it. And the shells, God's love, were scattered from my heart to where they could be distributed widely.

H = Hold On to the Self-Forgiveness When I Doubt That It Was Real

The fifth day I took the final step to REACH emotional self-forgiveness. *H* stands for holding on to self-forgiveness when I doubt that I have forgiven myself. I had found that in dealing with unrealistic expectations and now going through the five steps of REACH, I finally felt free.

But I knew I would have my doubts in the future. Those doubts would invade my emotional life, probably in times of great stress, times when my guard was down. So I knew I had better hope for the best and plan for the worst.

Freedom from stress, illness, or pain doesn't mean I'll never experience stress, illness, and pain again. And freedom from self-blame and shame doesn't mean I'll never experience those things again. If I believed this struggle was completely over, I would be setting myself up for disappointment, failure, and doubt.

I had a powerful image in seeing the sand leveled out and the shells drop down to touch the coral, representing my heart. I could use that memory to remind myself that I had been forgiven by God and myself. I also knew that I had been taught valuable lessons going through that process. I could review the lessons whenever I doubted. That could help me hold on to self-forgiveness whenever self-blame would bombard me.

Through all of these efforts at dealing with self-blame, I had been trying at the same time to reconcile with God. The two, I knew, were intertwined. We know that we are ambassadors of reconciliation, reconciling others to God as we have been reconciled to God (see 2 Corinthians 5:18–20). That indeed was what I felt like I had been experiencing. I was reconciling with God as I emotionally forgave myself by working through the steps to REACH emotional self-forgiveness.

Escape from the Prison of Self-Condemnation

As a crucial part of my plan to prevent—or to short-circuit—self-blame whenever it tried to get its nose under the edge of the tent again, I thought systematically about the lessons of freeing myself from self-condemnation. Along with receiving forgiveness from God (Step 1) had come gratitude, and I had decided to forgive myself. Out of my gratitude to God, I was motivated to make amends by helping straighten out Mike and Charlene's finances (Step 2). I had dealt with many of the faulty perfectionistic standards and had reduced rumination (Step 3). I had even weathered the challenge of Jane's suicide, and shortly afterward had experienced the joy of emotional self-forgiveness solidified by the experience at Jupiter Beach (Step 4). I still felt that I did not have a good handle on self-acceptance (Step 5), and it probably had a lot to do with some of my struggles with God. But I was moving in the right direction. Now I could see the doorway standing open, leading the way out of prison.

A Mennonite peace worker from Notre Dame University named John Paul Lederac said, "You do not build a bridge starting in the middle.

You start with a strong foundation on each shore, build toward the middle. When it is solid, others can walk across."[2] In the process of reconciling with God, we are responsible to take the step off our side onto the bridge. God will do the major bridge-building.

In looking back, I realize that reconciliation with God takes time and effort. We have to move step by step and keep moving forward, regardless of how tentatively we keep walking onto the span that God constructed. My initial steps onto the bridge happened when I wrote the book *Humility: The Quiet Virtue.*[3] I understood the importance of other people and of family in supporting us in times of weakness. I took another step when I decided to resume my morning devotional time instead of using the time for work. The devotions got me reconnected with God, and I began to enjoy spending time with God again. The next step farther onto the bridge was in my Florida retreat with God. My few little steps started me across that bridge. God is faithful, and he rushes to meet us more than halfway across. Reconciliation with God indeed was happening.

A NEW KIND OF TEST WAS COMING

When I returned to VCU for the fall 2008 semester, I started into the hectic academic year. This busyness was, I knew, going to be a different type of test. This was not going to be like Jane's suicide, which brought back old memories to haunt me. This was a test to see whether my reconciliation with God could withstand life's busy schedule.

We remember the parable of Jesus about the sower and seeds (see Matthew 13:1–23). The sower scattered seeds. Some fell on hard ground and couldn't take root. They baked in the sun and died. Some took root but were unable to really catch hold. Others took root well but were choked out by the familiar thorns, thistles, and kudzu of daily life. Some, however, fell on good soil. Those seeds grew healthy, putting down deep roots, and rising to become fine plants.

I did not want to be one of the seeds that seemed now to be promising and in good fellowship with God but had fallen among the thorns and thickets of normal, mundane life, which would choke out my spiritual life. That, I knew, was going to be the challenge.

Part 7

Step 5: Rebuild Self-Acceptance

17

How to Connect with God for Self-Acceptance

Live in the truth that you are deeply flawed and also valuable beyond belief

> Love yourself—accept yourself—forgive yourself—and be good to yourself, because without you the rest of us are without a source of many wonderful things.
>
> —Leo F. Buscaglia

Here is God's recipe for self-acceptance: you are flawed, but precious. The real struggle in gaining meaningful victory over self-blame is often not merely getting to the place where you can forgive yourself. As my experience shows, you can forgive yourself explicitly and still feel just as guilty and shamed about your misdeeds. The hardest struggle is accepting yourself as a flawed individual (we all are), and yet being convinced that you are precious to the Lord. Self-acceptance depends on two related processes: accepting your failure and accepting your value.

Accepting Your Failure

Accepting your failure means seeing that you will fail often and in ways you thought you were strong enough to avoid. You must recognize, and accept, that you are not as good a person as you'd like to believe.

I often have wondered why God didn't just get rid of the life of the flesh, the part of our nature that tends naturally to be self-seeking ahead of being kind, generous, patient, helpful, and so forth (see Philippians 3:3–4). Why didn't God replace the negative and destructive tendencies with the life of the Spirit—God's being alive within us and active in helping us (see Ephesians 5:18; 2 Timothy 1:7)? It seems that it would have been so much easier for all concerned. You and I would automatically consider God's desires first, before resorting to self-promotion or any approach that harms others. But that is not what God chose to do.

Instead of removing our natural bent toward pride and self-justification, God left that inclination intact and gave us God's Spirit as a Source of inner power and guidance. We are the ones who choose which influence to follow. As a result, life can seem a constant roller-coaster ride. A long, slow uphill climb to faith followed by a screaming, heart-stopping plunge into failure, followed by a slow climb back to faith. You have probably noticed the same patterns in the lives of now-famous biblical characters:

Thomas doubted Jesus's resurrection, but when Jesus invited Thomas to put his fingers in Jesus's wounds, Thomas was lifted from the valley of doubt to the pinnacle of belief. He said, without reservation: "My Lord and my God!" (John 20:24–29).

The disciples were so convinced that Jesus was the Messiah that they paraded him through the streets to shouts of Hosanna (see John 12:12–15). But in the Garden of Gethsemane, his disciples could not stay awake to support him in his most despondent moments; instead, they ran away when the crowd came to arrest Jesus (see Matthew 26:36–46, 56). But later their lives were transformed with the power of God's Spirit at Pentecost (see Acts 2:1–47).

In Matthew 16:13–19, Jesus asked his disciples who the crowds said he was. "Some say John the Baptist; others say Elijah…," they answered.

"But what about you?" he asked. "Who do you say I am?" Simon Peter answered, "You are the Christ, the Son of the living God." Jesus replied, "Blessed are you, Simon son of Jonah, for this was not revealed to you by man, but by my Father in heaven. And I tell you that you are Peter, and on this rock I will build my church, and the gates of Hades will not overcome it. I will give you the keys of the kingdom of heaven; whatever you bind on earth will be bound in heaven, and whatever you loose on earth will be loosed in heaven." But then we see an almost unbelievable about-face. On the heels of being affirmed by Jesus, Peter rebuked Jesus. And the Lord said to Peter: "Get behind me, Satan! You are a stumbling block to me; you do not have in mind the things of God, but the things of men" (verse 23). How could Peter plunge so quickly from the mountain of honor to the pit?

Immediately after that (see Matthew 17:1–13), Jesus took Peter, along with John and James, up a mountain. He allowed them to see him transfigured, talking with Elijah and Moses. Peter, in his impulsive way, blurted out his thoughts. He said, essentially, "Let's build shelters so we can stay here forever." This revealed once more how little Peter understood about Jesus, his mission on earth, and God's Kingdom. But once again, grace followed. God's voice announced to them, "This is my Son, whom I love; with him I am well pleased. Listen to him!" (verse 5).

At the Last Supper, Jesus took the bread and the cup and announced that his body and blood would be broken and shed for them. Imagine being present at the very first act of communion, with Jesus's fingers brushing your hand as he served you the bread and cup. That must have been a high spiritual moment! But notice what happened immediately following that. A dispute broke out over which of the disciples would be the greatest in the kingdom (see Luke 22:24–30). The disciples could move from spirit to flesh with astounding speed—about as quickly as I can.

Jesus then addressed Simon Peter: "I have prayed for you, Simon, that your faith may not fail. And when you have turned back, strengthen your brothers." But Simon avowed, "Lord, I am ready to go with you to prison and to death" (verses 32–33). Peter's confession of faith and loyalty, even to the point of death, is impressive. But this same Peter soon denied that he knew Jesus. And not once, but three times (verses 54–62). Yet we find that later Jesus restored Peter (see John 21:15–17).

We see a similar pattern in the words and lives of those God called to important service to him and to the world: tremendous faith and courage, followed by incredibly weak, stupid, unfaithful words and actions. Life with the Lord is not a steady spiritual peak experience. We do not reach progressively higher levels of maturity and righteousness. Instead, life and faith are a journey to a higher place that passes through many low valleys of sin and discouragement as well as through high mountains of faith and exuberance.

It seems to our eyes that it would have been better to have the faith and joy without the sin and suffering, to have the spirituality without the flesh. But the flesh and failure are there for a reason. We must learn that our connection with God is not a connection between equals. As the saying goes, there is one God and it's not me. Instead of relating face to face with God, we connect by clinging to God in utter dependence. How could we learn that and try, imperfectly, to practice it if we did not fail so often?

I have no choice but to believe the witness of Scripture and the truth of my own life. They confirm each other. And the facts are that I will continually mess up. I will fail in ways that are far worse than I ever thought possible. It is hard to accept, but I am like that. The weak flesh is always lurking beneath the surface. Yes, I can temporarily keep it at bay through faith and by staying close to Jesus. But I cannot kill it off. It will remain with me throughout my life on earth.

ACCEPTING YOUR VALUE

After we grasp our failure, our need, and our dependence on a trustworthy God, only then can we turn to the second half of self-acceptance: accepting our value. You have to encounter this truth and accept it fully: God knows you to be a fallible human who will keep failing all your earthly life. *Yet* while you are a sinner, God regards you of such unfathomable value that Jesus, beloved Son of God, died for you (see Romans 5:8).

Herein lies the real struggle in forgiving ourselves: how do we accept ourselves as valuable when we also accept that we are flawed, not just superficially but in a fundamental way? We bounce around morally like Ping-Pong balls in a wind tunnel. Yet we know as Christians that we have worth. Christ died for us.

This is not easy to understand or to grasp, much less to accept. But our lives prove it, and God's Word backs up that message. It is the truth, and to live and forgive as whole persons, we need to accept it in our heart of hearts.

In one of Jesus's shortest parables, he said, "The kingdom of heaven is like treasure hidden in a field. When a man found it, he hid it again, and then in his joy went and sold all he had and bought that field" (Matthew 13:44). In the following verse, Jesus says, "Again, the kingdom of heaven is like a merchant looking for fine pearls. When he found one of great value, he went away and sold everything he had and bought it."

While there are several ways to interpret these parables, I love the reading that says Jesus is the Man who found the treasure, and Jesus is the Merchant who found the pearl. Jesus discovered treasure and a pearl of great value—which is you, and me, and all people. For us, he paid everything he had—his earthly life. And he endured the silence of his Father for what must have seemed an eternity. We must be valuable indeed for the Creator of the universe to become a human; to endure life among deeply flawed, violent people; and to be willing to submit to human death for the eternal benefit of each of us.

We might understand in our heads that God accepts us, but that does not always make us feel acceptable to God in our hearts—especially if we have done shameful things. We must work to develop a sense of self-acceptance. It is not a rejection of God's grace to try to develop a good sense of self-acceptance—one that is informed by the Bible. We are not wrong when we agree with Jesus—that we are worth his life. He showed by his sacrifices that we were—even flawed and fallen—worth accepting.

Pastors, close friends, and family members can help you learn that you are valuable. Psychotherapists can also help. In fact, helping people be more self-accepting might be seen as the cornerstone of psychotherapy. People come to psychotherapists well aware of their flaws. Psychotherapists do not try to convince clients that they are perfect and sinless and that somehow the clients are imagining problems and weaknesses that simply are not there. Instead, psychotherapists help people be realistic about their fallenness and yet realize that they indeed have worth.

Viktor E. Frankl had been a psychotherapist. He was imprisoned in a Nazi death camp and was nearing the end of his strength, nourished only by a bowl of broth and piece of bread each day to fuel fourteen hours of hard labor. One day a prisoner stole some potatoes. The camp authorities demanded that the prisoners give the thief up so he could be hanged, or go hungry all day. "Naturally the 2,500 men preferred to fast," wrote Frankl. But near the end of the day, the prisoners were in their hut with hunger gnawing at their innards. Hope was at low ebb. Then the light failed and physical darkness mirrored their hopelessness. The senior block warden asked Frankl to talk to the men. I cannot hope to do his thoughts justice in my brief summary below. I urge you to read his talk in *Man's Search for Meaning: An Introduction to Logotherapy.*[1]

Frankl first asked the prisoners to think of what they had lost that they could not build up again. For most, the only things of value lost were other precious lives. Life had infinite meaning, including "suffering and dying, privation and death," he wrote.

> I asked the poor creatures who listened to me attentively in the darkness of the hut to face up to the seriousness of our position. They must not lose hope but should keep the courage in the certainty that the hopelessness of our struggle did not detract from its dignity and meaning. I said that someone looks down on us in difficult hours—a friend, a wife, somebody living or dead, or a God—he would hope to find us suffering proudly—not miserably—knowing how to die.[2]

In the darkest of situations, with men stripped of everything, the Jewish Frankl—even unable to appeal to "Christ in us, the hope of glory"—was able to get across the worth of the human. Stripped of position, of accomplishments, and of daily bread, the men were still of immense value. If they died, others who knew them—if asked what of value they had lost during the war—would have named those fellow prisoners who died as well as those who lived.

THE CONSISTENCY OF SELF-ACCEPTANCE

In chapter 6, I showed how self-condemnation is involved in our Self system. Self-blame often comes from detecting inconsistencies in your self-concept. You see yourself as well meaning and basically others oriented, but are confronted by your deeply flawed nature. Failure to accept yourself when (1) you don't live up to your expectations (that is, your concept of your real self falls far short of your ideal self) or (2) you see yourself as better than you are (that is, your self-concept includes a denial or a distortion of the harmful things you have done—refusing to admit bad things or inflating good things you have done).[3]

Self-acceptance is about living a consistent life. The results of any discrepancy between your disappointment over failing to achieve your expectations (that is, of a self-concept that falls short of your ideal self), or your tendency to deny the reality of your flawed life (the inaccuracies in your self-concept), and the truth about who you are as God sees you (your *true* self) are anxiety and plummeting self-esteem.

Let's revisit the ideal self for a moment with self-acceptance in mind. Remember, "ideal" in this case does not mean "perfect"; rather, it is the best we think we can do. We know that our ideal self, from a Christian standpoint, is as a flawed and dependent person. Our ideal self-concept is dependent not only on our actions and achievements (which, in thinking of Frankl's situation, we can see are temporal) but also on God working in us. God created us in his image, the *imago dei.* Being fallen by nature and doing wrong by choice, we have twisted that image. Yet it is still God's image shining out that gives our life value.

Our *real* self-concept is based on our real experiences, including departures from our ideal self. As we already discussed, self-blame and shame arise from those discrepancies—through inadequate behavior or a warped ideal self. If we become aware of those failings and do not try to correct our actions—either to repair the troublesome behavior or to modify our ideal self-concept to acknowledge our poor behavior—then self-condemnation will eat at us. But self-acceptance can be cultivated by consistently making ourselves aware of those departures and working to correct our behavior.

Accepting ourselves does not necessarily mean that we are satisfied with ourselves. It is simply resting in an accurate perception of our realistic self. Accepting ourselves means we understand that we are people who have followed life paths and those paths got us to the point where we are now. Acceptance is about being good enough—although we aspire to be better.

So we must be able to rest in the idea that we did things wrong before becoming Christians and we have done things wrong since becoming Christians. Having made a commitment to the lordship of Jesus, we are new creations (see 2 Corinthians 5:17). God's righteousness is imputed to us. We are people whom God sought out and whom God values (see 2 Timothy 1:9). At our creation, God had full knowledge of what we would be. We see from Psalm 139:13–18 that God knew us even in our mother's womb.

For me to accept myself is to realize that despite my flaws, I am a person intentionally created, loved, and wanted by God. Paul argues in Philippians 3:10–14 that we need to forget our past and move toward our destination. We are being pulled into the future, into a relationship with God that is going to stretch through eternity. So we are to forget our past and strain forward with a purpose.

In Romans 8:28, we read that all things work together for good for those who love God and are called according to God's purpose. Therefore we need to seek God's purpose and personal calling for us. Then we can rest in knowing that all things will ultimately work together for a good outcome. All the things I have failed at in my past, all the expectations I have not met, all the wrongs I have done—God will make them all work out for good in the end.[4]

I don't know how this happens. It's a mystery. But I do know we can trust God. Self-acceptance is based not on what you can do, but on what God can bring about in your life.

Self-acceptance involves giving mental assent to this reality (i.e., head

knowledge) and feeling it in your inner being (heart knowledge). Feeling it as heart knowledge is not easy, but you can make this truth an internal reality.

While God calls you valuable due to the value he places on you, you still have full responsibility to live as a person who seeks to do good in all things and to all people. You are responsible for the following:

- Trying to act virtuously in accord with your ideal self as you rely on God's power to do so.
- Confronting the truth of where you have fallen short of your ideal and confessing that to God (and sometimes to others).
- Correcting any ideals for your behavior that are impossibly high and clearly out of reach.
- Examining yourself honestly under the guidance of the Holy Spirit and identifying ways you tend to think too highly of yourself.
- Cultivating humility and squelching pride.
- Cultivating the assurance that God created you as valuable and will redeem you from failures if you seek God in faith.

Self-acceptance is not easy. If I could concretely describe in a short chapter exactly how you could achieve self-acceptance, I would be traveling to Stockholm to receive the Nobel Prize. All I can do is inadequately point you to these strategies and encourage you to try to meet the responsibilities and to trust that God is at work in you with real, miracle-working, transformative power.

18

How Emotional Self-Forgiveness and Self-Acceptance Make the Difference

A quick look at the life change that results

> Know that joy is rarer, more difficult, and more beautiful than sadness. Once you make this all-important discovery, you must embrace joy as a moral obligation.
>
> —André Gide

We all have options in dealing with self-condemnation. We can justify our actions, excuse our wrongdoing, take a defeatist approach by appealing to justice ("I deserve this suffering"), or let ourselves off the hook ("I don't deserve this suffering; I'm going to let it go").

In appropriate situations, employing such thinking might give you space and a little time to come to terms with facing up to your true self—the one that God knows but we so often don't want to know. We all know it's not easy to be confronted with the flaws in our self-concept—the ways in which we fall short of our idealized self. So giving ourselves a chance to get used to the truth of our flawed nature and actions can open the door to a deeper, healthier self-assessment.

But note that none of these alternatives to emotional self-forgiveness can move your emotions from negative to positive. These approaches are, at best, a temporary stage that will help ease you along a path toward the full freedom of self-forgiveness. They might serve, however, to move you from negative to neutral or negative to less negative. Or perhaps from shame to blame. As you get serious about considering your real self and begin to accept the sharp contrast between that self and your idealized self, you should be making an emotional shift that eventually will move you from negative to neutral to positive.

The Power of the Positive-to-Negative Ratio

When people move from self-condemnation to self-forgiveness and self-acceptance, their lives can't help but change—and usually in quite dramatic ways. I am convinced, although we have not studied this scientifically yet, that we will find an outcome that is very similar to findings of researchers working in other areas:[1] The shift will occur when positive thoughts outnumber the negative ruminations by a ratio of at least three to one. (Some say five to one.)

Here are examples of helpful positive thoughts: *There were benefits to the self-blame I've felt, and I can name them: It was a wake-up call, a motivation to seek change in my life, and preparation to take an even deeper, more clear-eyed look at myself. I can beat this self-blame. It was bad, but God is my Redeemer and will bring good out of this.* If that kind of thinking can outweigh negative ruminations, I believe you will notice a shift from self-blame to self-forgiveness and perhaps later to self-acceptance.

I had read things like this for years, but I finally put it together a couple of years ago when I gave a workshop on marriage. The audience included professional couple counselors, lay counselors, and people from the community. At lunch, Jorge and Rosalie approached me and asked if they could share some things with me. They are Mexican Americans, and at that time neither of them had been in the United States more than a few years.

Rosalie seemed more assertive in the partnership. "We like the things you've been teaching about hope-focused marriage," she said. "But I'm afraid we don't have much hope left for our marriage."

Jorge shuffled his feet. He didn't seem to feel comfortable about sharing their troubles. Then he interrupted Rosalie, saying, "Well, I don't think Rosalie is right. She exaggerates most of the time."

"You just try to deny the facts that are looking you right in the eyes," she said.

"Yeah, it is always your way," he said. "Your way or no way."

Rosalie looked at me. "You see what I have to put up with? He won't listen."

Of course I saw the problem. They had said nothing but negative things to me or to each other. After listening some more, I said, "Both of you seem to be unable to see the positive in each other or in your marriage. You said you don't have much hope left for your marriage. Yet you came to talk with me. You must be hoping for something."

Rosalie said, "You've seen a lot of marriages in counseling. I'm sure some people you've helped have more troubles than Jorge and I do. Do you think we can do anything to turn our marriage around?"

I looked at Jorge. "How about you? Do you want to turn your marriage around?"

"It is not something I would feel good about if we got a divorce. Our families would be disappointed in us. My mother is Catholic. Rosalie and I don't go to Mass, but Mama would be very disappointed. It would be hard to go home. I want to make our marriage work. But Rosalie, she is stubborn."

"And you're not!" Rosalie practically shouted. "You should be thankful for me as your wife. You should not be saying that it would be disappointing for *your family* if we got a divorce! You should be every day thanking God for me, not worried about what your family thinks."

"I see you both are hurt," I said. "You feel such pain that it makes you want to hurt and blame the other person. You feel each other's criticism. I know that hurts badly."

Rosalie teared up, but I continued. "I, of course, cannot counsel you. We live far from one another. And whatever I say in a few minutes over lunch will make little difference. I think that if you want to turn your marriage around, you need someone who will counsel you for several weeks."

"We don't have much money, though I have a good job," said Jorge. "We cannot afford an expensive counselor, and we don't belong to the church so we can't even go see the priest. Can't you tell us anything that might help?"

"I think there are counselors in your area who have sliding scales, so you would not have to pay a lot. To get back the love you used to have for each other, maybe for the rest of your lives, aren't you willing to invest in counseling? Will you promise me that you will look into this?"

"I'll see what I can find," Jorge said.

I looked from Jorge to Rosalie, and back to Jorge. "If I could tell you but one thing, with the understanding that you will seek counseling, it is this. Try to say only positive things to each other. Try not to be critical—or if you do, only once in a great while. And if your partner says something critical about you, try not to answer back with more criticism. If you feel like you can't help but answer back, at least try to wait one minute before you say anything negative."

"Is this so important," said Rosalie, "that we are positive with each other?"

"Yes, it is," I said. "No one can be one hundred percent positive. I'm sure that would not feel honest to you. But it is important that you change your relative amount of positives."

Jorge said, "Why is that important?"

"Negative emotions—especially deeply wounding negative emotions, such as contempt, disgust, and shame—are stronger than positive emotions," I said. "They take over your emotional lives. Once you allow negative emotions to rule your way of looking at each other, you will get stuck in a downward spiral of negativity. You will feel like you can't stop thinking negatively about the other person. So you have to take decisive action and do things that might at first feel inauthentic in order to break the negative patterns. Because negative emotions are so strong, the only way to deal with them is to outnumber them. You have to get at least a three-to-one advantage in favor of positive statements about and to each other, in order to win against the negative interactions."

"That makes sense," said Jorge.

"Will that help, though, trying to fake being positive?" Rosalie asked.

"You're right that at first it will feel artificial—even perhaps dishonest," I said. "Feeling like you're faking it in your comments won't be the thing that will bring about a change. But as you concentrate on being positive and finding positive traits in your spouse, you will notice that you are not arguing as much. That will have the near-immediate benefit of making you feel better about your marriage. It seems that you really do care for each other, so why not fight for your love? Trying to be more positive is not faking it when you still care for each other. It is trying to do a better job of showing that you care."

Jorge asked, "You think that will turn our marriage around?"

"Not right away," I said, "and maybe never. That is why I said you need to work with a counselor. But what happens is this: Sometimes there comes a point when things suddenly change emotionally. It is like moving a chair back onto just two legs." I stood and laid the chair I was sitting in onto its back.

"Suppose this chair is your marriage. It's not the way you'd like it to be. Working to be more positive is hard work. It is like lifting the chair." I slowly lifted it toward a more upright position, until it was almost balanced on its two back legs. I held it there by the slightest pressure of a finger.

"See, it took effort to move the chair from a stable, but horizontal, position to this unstable, but mostly upright, condition. The problem is, if I turn the chair loose I won't know which way it's going to fall. It might..."—I turned it loose and it crashed down to the floor—"ah, it might fall backward."

I lifted the chair and balanced it again. "But it might..."—this time I gave it a little nudge and it went to a stable sitting position—"it might right itself."

I could see they were engaging with this line of thinking, so I went on. "One marriage counselor, John Gottman, found that couples with five times as many positive interactions as negative ones were happy and their marriages lasted a long time.[2] In a different study, two psychologists found they could determine which business groups would work well together and which wouldn't.[3] Teams of employees that had at least three times as many positive interactions as negative worked well together. And in fact, some of these groups—those with a six-to-one ratio in favor of positive interactions—were super performers. One psychotherapist found that people who came to psychotherapy for help in overcoming depression at first registered ratios of one positive statement to every negative one—or even less.[4] By the end of counseling, the ratio was more than four positive to every one negative for clients who had improved the most."

"Well," said Jorge, "I have some hope. I'll try to be more positive if she will."

I looked at Rosalie. "It seems worth a try," she said.

THE FLIP FROM SELF-BLAME TO SELF-FORGIVENESS

Barbara Fredrickson, John Gottman, and many others have shown that many systems possess what has been called a tipping point. Journalist Malcolm Gladwell wrote an amazing book about such transformations.[5] I'll go out on a limb and say a tipping-point dynamic comes into play when people struggle with self-blame and shame. I predict that a dramatic shift can be experienced and that it will coincide with a stark change in the ratio of positive to negative ruminations. If you work effectively to shift your rumination from self-judgment and blame to telling your Self how valued it is to God and to others and that you bring unique value to the world and to those around you, you will approach a powerful tipping point in emotional self-forgiveness.

This is simple, but not easy. If you want to change your experience from self-blame to self-forgiveness and self-acceptance, decrease the negativity of self-blame and shame in your ruminations and increase the positivity of self-compassion, self-love, and especially recognizing that God loves you. It's not unlikely that over time, a tipping point and a spiritual transformation can occur.

FINDING YOUR VALUE IN GOD

Long-ago Archbishop of Canterbury William Temple said, "Humility does not mean thinking less of yourself than of other people, nor does it mean having a low opinion of your gifts. It means freedom from having to think about yourself at all."[6] Self-forgiveness frees us to shift our focus and live humbly for the benefit of others. It is only through the divine touch that you have life, meaning, and purpose on earth. Self-acceptance (Step 5) prepares you for the final step of the Six Steps to Self-Forgiveness (Resolve to Live Virtuously).

We began the journey of self-forgiveness by receiving grace and mercy from God (Step 1). Now, as we approach the end of the journey to freedom, we give ourselves grace and thus allow ourselves mercy when we will inevitably fail again. "It is for freedom that Christ has set us free" (Galatians 5:1).

You are worth God's love, and I hope you can accept yourself as one who is flawed but precious (Step 5). Whether you have conquered your self-blame and shame or whether you are at another place along the road to self-acceptance, you still are more valuable than any treasure.

I will close this chapter with a poem by Myra Brooks Welch, "The Touch of the Master's Hand." I hope it will be an inspiration to you.

THE TOUCH OF THE MASTER'S HAND

It was battered and scarred, and the auctioneer
Thought it hardly worth his while
To waste his time on the old violin,
But he held it up with a smile.

"What am I bid, good people," he cried,
"Who'll start the bidding for me?"
"One dollar, one dollar, Do I hear two?"
"Two dollars, who makes it three?"

"Three dollars once, three dollars twice,
Going for three"—but No!
From the room far back a gray-haired man
Came forward and picked up the bow.

Then wiping the dust from the old violin
And tightening up the strings,
He played a melody, pure and sweet,
As sweet as an angel sings.

The music ceased, and the auctioneer
With a voice that was quiet and low,
Said, "What now am I bid for this old violin?"
As he held it aloft with its bow.

"One thousand, one thousand. Do I hear two?"
"Two thousand. Who'll make it three?"
"Three thousand once, three thousand twice,
Going and gone," said he.

The audience cheered, but some of them cried,
"We do not quite understand."
"What changed its worth?" And swift came the reply.
"The touch of the master's hand."

And many a one with life out of tune,
All battered with bourbon and gin,
Is auctioned cheap by a thoughtless crowd
Just like that old violin.

A mess of pottage, a glass of wine,
A game, and he travels on.
He's going once. He's going twice.
He's going and almost gone.

But the Master comes, and the foolish crowd
Never can quite understand,
The worth of a soul and the change that is wrought
By the touch of the Master's hand.[7]

Part 8

Step 6:
Resolve to Live Virtuously

19

Live Virtuously, but Give Yourself Room to Fail

How your own self-forgiveness can benefit those around you

> They [children attending a school for needy youth] know what it took me decades to find out: to shine in secret and to give when there's no one applauding.... It's not too late to be inspired. It's not too late to change. It's not too late.
>
> —Andre Agassi

By the 2008–2009 academic year, I finally had experienced emotional self-forgiveness. I felt that I was being reconciled to God and was living closer to God. I had walked out the open prison door knowing I could not trust myself but needed to rely completely on Jesus. I had crossed the prison yard and accepted my imperfections. I had one final step to take to reach complete freedom—resolving to live virtuously but leaving myself room to fail.

I asked God to enable me to live as virtuously as possible. I did not want to fall back into perfectionism. So I knew it was important not just to practice the virtues to achieve some kind of ideal, but to practice cooperating with the Holy Spirit as a way of showing gratitude for the blessings I have received. But I also had to give myself mercy if I failed. The perfection God wants for us is an unreachable ideal within the span of our earthly life. It is intended not to create despair or striving for the impossible, but to create a goal that only can be pursued in humility by reliance on God.

Humility is a persistent theme of the Christian Scriptures. Paul, writing to the Philippians, stated:

> Your attitude should be the same as that of Christ Jesus:
>
> Who, being in very nature God,
>   did not consider equality with God something
>   to be grasped,
> but made himself nothing,
>   taking the very nature of a servant,
>   being made in human likeness.
> And being found in appearance as a man,
>   he humbled himself
>   and became obedient to death—even death on a cross!"
>   (Philippians 2:5–8)

Paul wrote with authority to the Christians at Philippi. He had been there before, so the people knew him. In fact, it is probable that sitting in the assembly as this letter was read was a Philippian jailer. His encounter with Paul was chronicled in Acts 16:16–36.

Paul and his partner Silas were in prison because they had cast a demon out of a slave girl, squelching her owners' plans for using her to amass wealth as a soothsayer. The owners had incited the authorities in Philippi against Paul and Silas. The two men were beaten and jailed. Around midnight an earthquake shook the jail and the doors flew open. The prisoners' chains fell off. The Philippian jailer awoke to find the doors standing open. Looking into the darkened and presumed empty cells, he drew his sword to kill himself out of shame and dishonor. Paul could have let the jailer commit suicide and then walked away clean, perhaps saying, "Ah, this was God's way of freeing us."

But he didn't. Paul called out, "Don't harm yourself! We are all here!" He sacrificed his freedom for the sake of the jailer.[1] Paul lived out the truth that he later wrote to the church at Philippi. He relied on God. He laid down his own freedom for the benefit of another person, even though it meant he would have to remain in jail. This is the humility that means true freedom. This was the true freedom that I desired.

True freedom is not absence from restraint, as many in modern culture think of it. Total absence of restraint can produce anxiety that inhibits our actions. True freedom is achieved in the security of dedication to a loving relationship. Within those boundaries, we can run free.

True freedom, then, can be experienced only if we try to stay closely connected with God. This requires prayer for self-control, a supportive network that helps us with self-control, and also our own efforts at self-control.

THE STORY BEHIND *THE MISSION*

Rodrigo Mendoza was a slave trader in Brazil. He made frequent raids into the high countries above the Iguazu Falls, carrying off men, women, and children who were sold into slavery on plantations in the lowlands. His true story was told in the movie *The Mission*. While Mendoza was on a raid, his lover fell in love with another man—Mendoza's brother, Felipe. Upon Mendoza's return, Mendoza killed his brother. He was eaten up by guilt over the killing and his slaving, and he went with some Jesuits to do penance.

In one of the most poignant ten-minute scenes ever filmed, Mendoza trailed the Jesuits up a mountain. He was too shame-burdened to merely climb the mountain. He insisted on dragging—at the end of a rope—a heavy bag of armor as an inadequate penance. When they finally reached the Guarani tribe, Mendoza struggled up the last incline with downcast eyes and drooping head, his reserves spent. He knew that his penance had not been enough. He tumbled to his knees with the bag of heavy armor anchoring him to earth. Worse, the Guarani realized who this bedraggled shell of a man was: the evil slave trader. A native grabbed a knife and ran at Mendoza. Mendoza awaited the attack with fatalistic surety.

The native grabbed Mendoza by the hair, jerked his neck back, and with incredible savagery, the native hacked the cord that had anchored Mendoza to the armor. His burden tumbled into the water, where it was washed away.

Mendoza wept. His penance and even the threat of his death had no power to set him free. But grace and mercy given to him from the Christian-converted natives had set him free at last.

In the movie *The Mission,* we see lessons portrayed that I had learned over the last few years. We see the power of God's redemption, especially visible when we fail. We see that effort on our own behalf will never fully set us free from guilt and shame—although it took Mendoza's effort to get him in the place where grace and mercy could set him free. His unrealistic expectation that he had to do "enough" penance to make up for his guilt and shame was finally corrected as a native slashed him free from his burden. He received emotional peace and experienced emotional self-forgiveness and self-acceptance as a gift from others. His work, building and maintaining the mission, was part of making amends and simultaneously living a virtuous life. In the end, he was able to give the ultimate sacrifice without trying to maintain his own virtue but, instead, trying in humility to save others.[2]

MY LIFE MISSION AND THE ROLE OF CONFESSION

Complete freedom from self-blame and shame meant, to me, to do what I felt was God's mission for me—to do all I could to promote forgiveness in every willing heart, home, and homeland—in as much humility as possible. Earlier I had let that mission statement become a dictator in my life; it drove me to workaholism. Now I could again pursue that mission, and if I had learned anything it was that I would most certainly fail often. Yet failure is not the end of the story.

God loves us. That is the end of the story. That is what frees us for future chapters as the narrative of our lives unfolds. We are admonished to love God above all. Ultimately, God is the Source of our healing. Jesuit Peter van Breemen, retreat organizer and spiritual director from Germany and author of *The God Who Won't Let Go,* puts it this way: "So long as we do not accept ourselves, we cannot be really free, especially in our relationships. That lack of self-acceptance will foster in us the tendency to be selfish, to try to bind others to ourselves, to cling, to take advantage of, and then, of course, to be disappointed time and time again, over and over."[3]

My testimony in *Moving Forward* is that God loves and thus heals. There are many ways to receive healing, but the ultimate source of all is through Jesus. We constantly face our wrongdoing. Our guilt mounts like a weight upon our shoulders, bearing us down, exhausting us, until we can become cynical. We can come to believe that, because we don't see any good in ourselves, there must be no good in people whatsoever. This is not the case, of course.

All of us fail. The sad thing is that despite how motivated we might be to act nobly, too often we fail to do even what we desire so badly to start doing. We stand by and let evil be done without lifting a finger. Or we passively fail to heed the call of God to act in behalf of others. Let's face it. We fail. We deserve blame and we know it in our hearts.

So when we fail, what do we do? God has made a way for us to be restored, of course. That is to confess our sins. Erwin W. Lutzer, author of a number of helpful books and pastor of Moody Church in Chicago, said, "Forgiveness is always free. But that doesn't mean that confession is always easy. Sometimes it is hard, incredibly hard. It is painful to admit our sins and entrust ourselves to God's care."[4]

We can't scrupulously confess everything we've done wrong. Even when we buck up our nerve and confess, we cannot delude ourselves that we have confessed all of our sins. God doesn't expect it. Every act of confession is, in a way, a symbolic act. What we confess *stands for* many things we did not confess. God knows what we need and will "purify us from all unrighteousness" (1 John 1:9).

We have probably all had the experience of having a great time of confession to the Lord. We believe we really opened ourselves to God's scrutiny. And yet, even in the glow of having thoroughly confessed, we sense that (if we look hard enough) we only skimmed the surface. There is so much more we could have confessed.

A GOD WHO WON'T LET GO

In *The God Who Won't Let Go,* van Breemen characterizes our guilt as an iceberg, 90 percent of which is below the surface of our awareness with only 10 percent visible. Perhaps a wave of devotion sloshes back the waters and for an instant we see that our guilt extends far beyond what we have seen before. We know and we delight that we have more confession and repentance ahead because we know that if we expose the icy guilt to the sun, it will melt away.

> There are always people who swim around the iceberg and try to lift it.... What one gains on one side, one loses on the other.... God does not want us to do something so unhealthy, neither does the church require it from us. It is enough to acknowledge and confess what we are aware of.... The sacrament of reconciliation lies in God's forgiveness, not in our examination of conscience, nor in our confession. There is a real danger in confession becoming deformed or distorted to the point where God is no longer the focus.[5]

Van Breemen reminds us that healing comes from God, not from our own efforts. We know this is true. Yet we also know that Jesus left his disciples (at the end of the gospel of Matthew) with two great lessons: the Greatest Commandments and the Great Commission. The Greatest Commandments are given to us in Matthew 22:37–40.

> Jesus replied: " 'Love the Lord your God with all your heart and with all your soul and with all your mind.' This is the first and greatest commandment. And the second is like it: 'Love your neighbor as yourself.' All the Law and the Prophets hang on these two commandments."

Jesus also left his disciples with the Great Commission (Matthew 28:19–20).

> Therefore go and make disciples of all nations, baptizing them in the name of the Father and of the Son and of the Holy Spirit, and teaching them to obey everything I have commanded you. And surely I am with you always, to the very end of the age.

These admonitions are not pietistic or passive. They encourage us to have the greatest of faith and yet to act powerfully and purposefully, motivated by love of God and others. But the Scriptures clearly tell us, life is not all about our own peace. We are called to a noble purpose. God has created us for great acts so that we may accomplish acts of love, altruism, and blessing for others. God says, when we are weighed down with guilt and shame, "Rise. Be healed. Go. Surely I am with you always." Self-condemnation is finally swept away, blown by the breath of God. We inhale freedom. We exhale virtue and its siblings, gratitude and love.

Part 9

In Closing

20

Life-Changing Lessons About Forgiving Yourself

The practical benefits of making things right

> On our own strength, we are not capable of really forgiving, especially if it concerns deep hurt. Forgiving is the most divine thing we can do. It is the completion of love. When we notice that we cannot (yet) forgive, we must be very much on our guard not to blame ourselves or to get discouraged, so long as there is a sincere desire to grow towards forgiveness.
>
> —Peter van Breemen

There is no one acceptable path that takes you to the place where finally you can forgive yourself. My experience, as you have seen, progressed step-by-faltering step as I lurched along toward self-forgiveness. This is one of the most demanding and difficult journeys any of us will attempt.

Important Lessons on the Road to Self-Forgiveness

My experience of being set free from self-condemnation led me through a prison where cell doors would open and then close. Many times I thought I had completed the process and could walk out through the prison gate, never to return to self-blame, condemnation, and guilt. But then I would come to another locked door, and again I would have to search for the key to make possible the next step toward freedom.

Here are some of the lessons I drew from my experiences. These will differ in the details from your journey, but I am convinced that the stages in the process are very similar for all of us.

Self-forgiveness is a doorway, not a destination

Self-forgiveness is not the end of all experience. It is not merely aimed at getting rid of your bad feelings. Rather, it is part of what helps you connect and stay connected intimately with the Lord, and through that to connect with others. Living in intimacy with God, with all of its ups and downs, is the destination we are seeking.

You cannot conquer trauma

Instead of being mere conquerors of life's traumas, we walk through trauma with someone beside us. This view goes against the Bruce-Willis-*Die-Hard*-American tradition of facing and subduing our enemies on our own. But I learned that trauma is less a problem to solve than it is a journey of self- and God-discovery. It is an invitation to explore yourself in relation to others and to your Creator. Many other people helped me. Maureen Miner, by listening and asking pointed questions, got me thinking differently. My wife, Kirby, walked with me quite literally every step of the way. Others came alongside briefly, just as I had walked beside the frustrated woman who couldn't run marathons. Those are divine appointments. If we are alert and open to them, then we can receive (and give) help.

The journey helps us, and it puts us in places where we can help others. All along the way, if we are open to it, we are gaining wisdom as we learn life lessons and develop life skills that move us toward self-forgiveness. Defeating trauma and leaving it behind for good is not the goal. Real traumas have a way of coming back, like bad movies on late-night television. We don't kill traumas; we move through them and, when they do broadside us, we call on the help that got us through them the first time—God and our closest friends and supporters. So a big lesson I learned was that we don't conquer trauma. We *more than* conquer trauma. We walk through trauma connected with God and with the people God brings across our paths.

Look for spiritual connections in unlikely places

Think back to stories in the Bible about people who have impressed you—either for their great faith or their struggles with faith. How often have you read about those who connected with God in places of darkness, death, and trials? Those are the places where real spiritual work is done. Jesus was raised from the dead in a dark, dank grave after being tested in a dark, damp garden, deserted by all the friends he had on earth. He was publicly humiliated and executed as a criminal, though he did nothing wrong.

Daniel was undeservedly thrown into a lions' den, and God kept the mouths of the lions closed as the prophet spent a night in darkness surrounded by death (see Daniel 6). Daniel's friends Shadrach, Meshach, and Abednego (see Daniel 3) were thrown into a furnace so hot that it consumed the men who had thrown them in. Yet someone walked with the men in the furnace and kept them from being scorched—someone, as Nebuchadnezzar said, who looked like "a son of the gods" (verse 25). And we won't even *think* about the prophet Jonah, marinated in gastric juices while touring a fish's digestive system.

Spiritual connection can happen where we think no spiritual connection is possible. Yet often those places serve as crucibles. It is there that we feel the darkness, the pressure, and the heat. Those are the places where God is working to mold us into people who are conformed into Christ's image.

Stay in contact with God and with others

Don't be like me. I withdrew when I felt the heat and the fear. But when I pulled away from others, I was working against myself. I needed to stay in contact with God and be open to the input and care of people who were concerned. As long as I struggled, God could work and others could be there for me. Sometimes our struggle is crying, "Where are you, God?" At least then we are seeking God's presence.

God is always available

God is always with us through the darkness of the grave, the smell and the fear of the lions, and the heat and the smoke of the fire. I had read the well-known stories in the Bible many times, but when it was my life and guilt that I was wrestling with, I did not always see God. In fact, there were times when I was not looking for God. Yet God did not turn me loose. Even back then I suspected it because I kept running into people who called me back to look for God. My community of friends and family, and even Christians who were only acquaintances, were essential to my journey. With them involved, I could not take what seemed to be the easy way and just quit on God.

Defeat can help you—if you let it

It is never fun to encounter obstacles. We must exert effort to surmount them. But for me, the times when I realized I could not solve my problems were wake-up alarms. Those failures slowed me down long enough to reconsider where I was in the process and triggered me to seek God to find out what was going on. Discomfort forced me to look for the patterns that God was laying out. Desperation made me willing to accept the patterns so that I might be able to get over self-blame and lack of self-acceptance.

THE BIG LESSON: GOD IS IN CONTROL

Each of the lessons above points to a great, overarching lesson: God is in control. If only I could always practice that, life would be filled with much more deep joy.

In March 2009 I had a chance encounter in Chicago's O'Hare Airport, waiting for a flight home after participating in an all-morning workshop. I was working away, sitting in a corner away from the foot traffic. It was the best spot to avoid interruption. I was laboring over a writing project and was thinking of incorporating part of Immaculée Ilibagiza's story in it. Immaculée is a beautiful Rwandan woman who, during the one hundred days of terror in which eight hundred thousand Rwandans were murdered by their kin and neighbors, had hidden in a bathroom with six other women. In that crowded room, as the women wondered if they would be discovered and butchered, Immaculée closely encountered God. Her message, told in the book *Left to Tell: Discovering God Amidst the Rwandan Holocaust,*[1] is that forgiveness comes by the grace of God.

At the airport, as I considered whether to include the brutal yet redemptive story in one of the journal articles I was writing, an African American woman in her twenties dropped into the seat next to me. She asked what I was reading.

"It's a real-life adventure about a woman chased by a mob in Rwanda. The woman came to know God better as a result. She learned how to forgive people who had tried to kill her."

The young woman's eyes flashed in fear, then a tear tumbled onto her blouse. Her reaction was so extreme that I couldn't just retreat back to my manuscript.

"What's wrong?" I asked her.

"Nothing," she said.

"I don't want to pry if you don't want to tell me, but that was quite a reaction to a ten-second book summary."

At this, the young woman started crying full out. She fumbled in her purse for some tissue. She covered her face, wiped the tears, and blew her nose. Then she said, "You look safe." She started crying again.

I waited her out. After a few minutes she went through her tissue ritual again. "I've been on the run since New Year's. I've been all over the States. I got involved in some bad stuff. Drugs. Other stuff to get the money for drugs. The guy I was living with—well kinda living with 'cause he gave me an apartment and came over all the time—beat the crap out of me, so I took off. I knew some stuff he had done. Bad stuff, not just the drugs and the ladies. Some *really* bad stuff. Anyway, I found out he was looking for me. He told my lady friend he was going to 'take care of me,' if you know what I mean. I knew too much about him.

"I had enough money to get the bus out of town. Been on the run since then. I know he's still looking for me 'cause I call my friend once in a while."

This was not the usual airport conversation, and I hadn't heard stories like that since my early days of counseling with clients in a drug and alcohol rehabilitation program. "You're heading to Richmond?" I asked.

She looked wary. "Passing through. Earned enough in Chicago that I can afford to fly. Got a friend down south of Richmond near North Carolina. Can't tell you where. She's going to drive up and meet me. I'll hide out at her place for a while."

"Sounds like you should be talking to the police."

"They ain't my friends. They'd put me in prison for the things I do—drugs and men and stuff. Anyway, I'm tired of living the life. Been living it for ten years since I done run away from home. I'm ready to get righteous. Tell me about that forgiveness book. I have a lot of people I need to forgive."

"A Rwandan woman named Immaculée—I actually met her last June in Nassau—hid out—"

"Cool," she said. "You actually met someone who writes books."

"Yes. She hid out, even though people had killed her brother and other family members. They hacked them to death with machetes. When she was hiding, she met God closely and it changed her life. She went from being an uncommitted Catholic to someone who knew God deeply and knew God loved her and would protect her. And she had the faith to accept that even if it was her time to go, to meet her earthly end like her brother had, God would be with her in her suffering and would forgive her. She felt that if God could forgive her, she ought to forgive the people who were hunting her. After the violence ended, she looked up some of those people and told them she forgave them."

"No way I could do that," the young woman said. "For one thing, God couldn't forgive me for all the stuff that I done."

"I know he could," I said. "I have been wrestling with forgiving myself for the last few years. God has forgiven me. And last summer I was even able to forgive and accept myself."

"An old white guy like you. Ha. No offense, but you ain't got nothing to forgive yourself for. You don't know what it's like, living in fear, getting money for sex, hunting your next fix." She was wearing a braided hairpiece. I remember noting that it was slipping, unnoticed, off to the side of her head.

"You're right. I don't know that world at all. It seems very hard." She started crying again. As I talked, she bobbed her head forward and wiped ineffectually at her nose. The hairpiece slipped further. She reached up and tugged it free, leaving her hair disheveled. I said to this fellow traveler: "I did have a lot of guilt after my brother killed himself because he couldn't get the images of our mother's murder out of his mind."

The young woman was thoughtful. "Did you get any peace in forgiving yourself? 'Cause I could use some peace."

"Yeah, I did. And, although I sure don't have a story like yours, I felt pretty bad about myself for a long while. I even ran from God."

An airline attendant had begun to board passengers for the flight to Richmond. I shuffled my papers, looking for my boarding pass. "Are you on this flight?" I asked.

"Maybe. Standby. So how did you do it? How did you forgive yourself?"

"One of the hardest parts was confessing my sins and failings to God."

"Yeah, that would take me the next few years. What next?"

"I couldn't get any peace for a long time because I didn't see how I could do anything to even slightly make up for things I'd done. I hadn't been able to stop my brother from killing himself even though I was a psychologist…"

"Dannnggg," she drawled. "A real psychologist. My lucky day." The airline attendant was about to call Zone 5. I didn't have much time.

"So, I finally realized I couldn't help my brother, Mike—that was water over the dam with him already dead—but I could help others, like his wife and kid and maybe even other people, like you, who are struggling to forgive themselves."

"Well, I can't make up for the stuff I done. That's for sure. So God won't be able to love me."

"God loves you already. God thinks you are a worthy person whether you make up for things you've done wrong or not. You know, Jesus died…"

"Yeah, yeah. I was brought up in a Catholic school myself. I know the Jesus-died-for-your-sins stuff. Don't be witnessing to me."

"You're right. I couldn't help but think of the woman that the crowd caught in adultery…"

"I remember that one."

"Do you remember what happened?"

"I think that's where Jesus wrote in the dirt, right?" I nodded. "All the crowd dropped their rocks and walked away," she said, saying this halfway as a question.

"Do you remember what Jesus said to her?"

"Not really."

"He said something like, 'Where are the people accusing you? Neither do I condemn you. Go and sin no more.'"

"I remember," she said. She got quiet and thoughtful. "So you felt that God forgave you and you could do other good stuff to help people. Did that make you forgive yourself?"

"Actually, I had to make a conscious decision to forgive myself, and then it took quite a while after that. Finally, I could be compassionate enough toward myself that I *felt* that I had forgiven myself."

"But you made it, huh?"

"I'm at peace now. But it took awhile to be able to accept myself—in addition to forgiving myself—as a person who could fail his own brother."

The final call was being made to board the plane. "I have to go," I said.

"Thanks for talking to me. You gave me a lot to think about," she paused, "even if you couldn't save me."

"I hope you make the next flight," I said over my shoulder. "And I hope you find the peace you're searching for."

Steps to Self-Forgiveness

Over three years I haltingly went through the Six Steps to Self-Forgiveness. It's not essential to move through the steps exactly as I have laid them out. You might go through the steps quickly, slowly, or in a different order. You might skip steps or add your own. Still, this is a basic plan for conquering self-condemnation and forgiving yourself. So let's review the steps in summary.

When you are unforgiving toward yourself, it often yields a sense of isolation. You tell yourself that if you can't forgive yourself, neither can anyone else, including God. But you are not alone. Jesus is with you in the fiery furnace. You will need to go to God to deal with the messages you keep sending yourself—the ruminations. You need to recognize up front how you might be making the problems worse. Decide to deal with it. Today you will begin the path to forgiving yourself.

Step 1: Receive God's forgiveness

When you go to God, confess explicitly your wrongdoing—both the ways that you have failed to act and the ways that you have acted wrongly. Confess your lack of faith in getting bogged down in self-blame. Then rest assured that if you confess your sins, God is faithful and just to forgive your sins and purify you from all unrighteousness (see 1 John 1:9). Accept God's forgiveness and rest in God's peace.

Step 2: Repair relationships

When you have done wrong or fallen short of your standards, often it has involved you doing harm to other people. Try to make things right. Sometimes you will go to the person you have harmed and confess your wrongdoing, apologize, and make restitution. At other times you won't be able to locate the person, or she has died, or it might not be wise to go to others because it might create more problems than it solves. In those cases, make indirect amends by making yourself available to assist others who suffer from wrongs done to them.

Step 3: Rethink ruminations

Ruminations are the thoughts that occupy your mind, and they tend to be condemning thoughts that feed self-blame and prevent self-forgiveness. Combat rumination by determining why your unrealistic expectations do not square with reality and with everyday life. Then try to deal with each one. Determine what realistic expectations look like, and use methods that come from cognitive therapy and from historic church practices to replace your ruminations with positive, hopeful, constructive thinking.

If you focus on God or on others, you'll realize that the chatter in your head occurs less often. You will have reduced rumination.

Step 4: REACH emotional self-forgiveness

Work through the five steps captured in the acrostic REACH, which lead to emotional self-forgiveness:

1. *Recall* the hurt.
2. *Empathize* with yourself by considering the reasons that you disappointed yourself.
3. Give yourself the same *altruistic* gift you would give other people—understanding and forgiving.
4. *Commit* to the emotional self-forgiveness that you experience in order to...
5. *Hold on* to self-forgiveness if you ever doubt that you have forgiven yourself.

By working through the five steps to emotional self-forgiveness, you can experience the emotional healing that can complete your sense of peace. Given the impossibility of doing this on your own, commit yourself to be dependent on Jesus as you do this difficult work.

Step 5: Rebuild self-acceptance

Self-acceptance is often the aspect of self-forgiveness that is the most difficult. We must adjust our self-concept to acknowledge that we behaved in ways we find abhorrent. In the past we believed that we were not the type of people who would be hurtful or damaging toward others. But in the first five steps to self-forgiveness, we acknowledged our wrongdoing and failure to live as virtuously as we would like. We now accept ourselves as fallen and flawed people, but at the same time acknowledge that we are enormously valuable to the Lord.

Step 6: Resolve to live virtuously

By moving through this time of struggle and forgiving and accepting yourself, you will want to live a virtuous life. On one hand, you won't want to go through self-condemnation again. But you can also emotionally understand that God has rescued you from the pit. Out of gratitude, you can strive to act virtuously, support others, love others, and give to others—all in the grace of God.

The process continues, even after you have worked through the six steps. Realize that you will fail. There are times when you will be imperfect, failing to meet your expectations. You cannot eradicate your flaws, even after you have determined you will live close to God. But God is gracious and merciful and will forgive, and Jesus is your Redeemer. Those errors and failings can be redeemed and used for good. So give yourself space to fail and the knowledge that God will work things out for a good outcome (see Romans 8:28).

Making Your Own Way

The six steps are not a recipe leading to surefire defeat of self-blame and shame and thus guaranteeing an uninterrupted happy life. The steps are suggested processes that many people have used to find forgiveness from God and others and to forgive themselves. The steps set us on a positive, productive path.

I hope that by now you are looking at the prison of self-blame and shame as a receding speck in your rearview mirror. As you drive into the distance to act virtuously toward others, remember with thankfulness to God that the chains of self-condemnation no longer bind you. I hope you never again have to use these skills. Even though you may hurt someone or do not live up to your own expectations or even godly standards, I pray that you never again will become imprisoned by the chains of self-blame and shame.

And through your journey, remember Galatians 5:1: "It is for freedom that Christ has set us free."

TAKING YOUR OWN STEPS

This guide is designed to help you continue your journey of forgiving yourself. Keep a notepad nearby so you can write down your thoughts, plans, questions, and next steps.

1. Everett L. Worthington Jr., writes that it is more difficult to forgive yourself than to forgive others. How do you feel about his statement?

2. The author shares in detail his deepest regrets over his relationship with his late brother. How important is it to be this transparent about your failures? Would you agree this is a necessary step in the process of self-forgiveness?

3. It is natural to condemn yourself for your words and actions that hurt others. In your struggle with self-condemnation, has God appeared to be more often a helper and comforter or a judge? Do you believe God can help you change self-condemning patterns? What assumptions and habits have you identified that prevent God from helping you let go of self-condemnation?

4. You begin to forgive yourself when you make a firm decision to do so. Write down your commitment to do this, then tell someone you trust about your decision. (This person can serve as an accountability partner.) It also helps to write your decision on a card and post it where you will see it regularly. Are you ready to take this step?

5. Clear away major obstacles by first seeking divine forgiveness. List the ways in which you have wronged others, yourself, and God. Also include things you should have done but failed to do. Next, pray to God, seeking God's forgiveness for each of the things you have written down.

6. If you have confessed to God the words and actions that give rise to your self-condemnation, as well as the failures to act, consider 1 John 1:9. If you confess your sins, God is faithful and just to forgive your sins and to purify you. Can you accept God's forgiveness? If not, why not?

7. After you have received God's forgiveness, consider whether to go to those you have wronged, if that is possible and if it would not lead to further harm. Choose one wrong you are dealing with. Write a good confession and practice saying it aloud. (However, if making this confession to the wronged party would harm that person further, you need to confess to God alone or to a trusted person such as a pastor or your spouse. The same is true if the person is no longer living, cannot be located, or has refused to listen to you.) Do you want to confess to the person?

8. If you decide to confess to the person you harmed, are you ready to do so? If not, why not?

9. Is restitution appropriate? Think of reasons it would be helpful to make amends to the wronged party for what you did or said that was harmful. If it's possible and appropriate, what would be meaningful restitution in this instance? It might be best to ask directly, "What can I do to make up for what I have done?"

10. If you have made things right with God and have done what is possible, advisable, and safe to make things right with others, you can forgive yourself. If you have made that decision, write it down. This is what the author calls "decisional self-forgiveness." It is an essential step toward finding peace. (To experience complete *emotional* self-forgiveness, continue to work through the following questions. It is possible to replace negative emotions toward yourself with positive emotions.)

11. You can replace negative, unforgiving emotions with empathy, compassion, and love. This is not easy, as you already know. You are the offending party, so you are doing this work to forgive a wrongdoer—yourself. To help you succeed, seek the help of people who know you well and who love you. Write down the names of three close friends or trusted advisors who will help you. (To work fully through the five steps of emotional self-forgiveness captured in the acronym REACH, go to chapter 16 of this book.)

12. Which is stronger, your sinfulness or God's grace? Write a brief description of a time you experienced the impact of God's grace through your entire being. How can you rely on the power of God's grace in times when you realize you are slipping back into patterns of self-blame, condemnation, and lack of self-acceptance?

13. The author says that self-acceptance can be harder than forgiving yourself. Is this in line with your experience? Can you accept yourself as deeply flawed in a fundamental way and yet know that God loves you very much and thinks you are precious?

14. Because God loves you, you might want to try to be even more dedicated to honoring God through virtuous behavior. Would you like to dedicate yourself to some specific virtue right now? You can write yourself a commitment just below.

15. Has God set you free from the prison of some of your past as you worked through these six steps to self-forgiveness? If so, have you expressed your gratitude?

ACKNOWLEDGMENTS

In a book as autobiographical as this one, it would be redundant to name each person and the contribution he or she made. While I used my story to frame the lessons about getting free from self-blame and shame, the important thing is not my story. I wrote this book to help *you.*

I have tried to write as a participant-observer, which tied together my life as an imperfect and struggling Christian man. But I also wrote as a psychological scientist, a clinician, and one who now trains other psychotherapists and couple therapists. I have observed many people struggle with self-condemnation. They have taught me much of the nobility of the human spirit and how pain and suffering can dampen the flame but not extinguish it. Let me mention a few people who acted behind the scenes to make this book possible. I have worked with numerous talented and bright students, and all have helped in their way. Michael Scherer and Katie Campana wrote dissertations on self-forgiveness, and Katie did her thesis on it too. Working through their research helped immeasurably. Donnie Davis and Joshua Hook also have worked hard on many of the topics I have dealt with—notably humility, forgiveness, and Christian psychology. I also had the privilege to cowrite an article with Diane Langberg on self-forgiveness and complex trauma as it applied to veterans and soldiers.

Research on self-forgiveness is part of my program of research on forgiveness specifically and on the virtues more generally. I try to understand these both from a secular and a Christian point of view. Two funding agencies have aided me in this research—the Fetzer Institute and the John Templeton Foundation. This understanding of self-forgiveness would not have occurred without the support of those foundations. I am extremely grateful.

A few people deserve special thanks. Dr. John M. (Jack) Templeton Jr. is, as far as I am concerned, the world's single greatest benefactor of research on forgiveness. He is president of the John Templeton Foundation, which carries out the intent of his father, Sir John, but he also has personally donated countless dollars and hours to funding and securing funding for forgiveness research—my own and others'. Wayne Ramsey was for years the program officer supervising our research on forgiveness. Wayne has blessed me for years with his intellect and gentleness.

My colleagues in research, including past and present students, have challenged me and provided the context to put ideas to the scientific test. My work would be much less meaningful without the community at our church. My gratitude toward Kevin Germer and the many people at Christ Prez is deep and sincere.

This book also could not have come about without valuable help from my agent, Esmond Harmsworth (Zachary Shuster Harmsworth), who encouraged me and gave valuable suggestions on how to express myself in a way that you might both enjoy and be blessed by. Then, the top flight team at WaterBrook Multnomah, headed by Ron Lee, helped refine the writing further. Any weaknesses in writing are almost certainly because I stubbornly did not heed their suggestions. Finally, I hope you'll visit my website for additional resources (ForgiveSelf.com). It was very ably constructed by Steven Hansel at Hansel Consulting LLC (steve@hanselconsulting.com).

I am grateful to my four adult children, who continue to amaze and delight me. I can freely share my life with them, and they share their lives with Kirby and me. In particular, Becca and Christen (Hansel)—two of my four children—have helped with this book by applying their considerable editing talents to the manuscript. Thank you, Christen and Becca. You've made a huge difference.

Although I have spoken often about my wonderful and fulfilling forty-two-plus-year marriage relationship with Kirby, I must say this: My precious one, you have helped me more and in more ways than I can possibly remember or ever acknowledge. I appreciate all of your support, your example, and your teaching. I hope we will be even more in love after our next forty-two years of marriage.

I am extremely grateful for the many blessings I have received through the journey that moved me forward from self-condemnation along the Six Steps to Self-Forgiveness. I could not have done it alone.

Learn more about how to move forward and break from the bondage of self-shame and guilt at www.ForgiveSelf.com.

NOTES

Chapter 1

1. *Les Misérables* has been presented in various forms on stage and on screen. The dramatic performances are based on Victor Hugo's historical fiction, first published in French in 1862 and considered a classic of nineteenth-century literature. To read Hugo's moving exploration of the nature of law and grace, see Victor Hugo, *Les Misérables,* unabridged ed. (New York: Signet Classics, 1987).

Chapter 2

1. Everett L. Worthington Jr., *Forgiving and Reconciling: Bridges to Wholeness and Hope* (Downers Grove, IL: InterVarsity Press, 2003).
2. Worthington, *Forgiving and Reconciling.*
3. Nathaniel G. Wade, William T. Hoyt, and Everett L. Worthington Jr., "Meta-analysis of Psychotherapeutic Interventions to Promote Forgiveness" (unpublished manuscript, October 5, 2012).
4. Everett L. Worthington Jr., Charlotte Van Oyen Witvliet, Pietro Pietrini, and Andrea J. Miller, "Forgiveness, Health, and Well-being: A Review of Evidence for Emotional versus Decisional Forgiveness, Dispositional Forgivingness, and Reduced Unforgiveness," *Journal of Behavioral Medicine* 30 (2007): 291–302.

Chapter 3

1. *The Power of Forgiveness,* written and directed by Martin Doblmeier, Journey Films, 2007.

2. Corrie ten Boom, *The Hiding Place,* with John Sherrill and Elizabeth Sherrill (Grand Rapids, MI: Chosen Books, 1971), 217.
3. *The Hiding Place* (movie adaptation), directed by James F. Collier, written by Allan Sloane and Lawrence Holben, WorldWide Pictures. 1975.
4. *Good Will Hunting,* directed by Gus Van Sant, written by Ben Affleck and Matt Damon, Miramax Films, 1997.
5. Lewis B. Smedes, *Shame and Grace: Healing the Shame We Don't Deserve* (New York: HarperCollins, 1993), 154.
6. Jonathan Aitken, *John Newton: From Disgrace to Amazing Grace* (Wheaton, IL: Crossway Books, 2007).
7. *Pretty Woman,* directed by Garry Marshall, written by J. F. Lawton, Touchstone Pictures, 1990.
8. Lewis B. Smedes, *The Art of Forgiving* (New York: Ballantine Books, 1996), 178.

Chapter 4

1. Viktor E. Frankl, *Man's Search for Meaning: An Introduction to Logotherapy* (New York: Pocket Books, 1963), 104.

Chapter 5

1. Everett L. Worthington Jr., Charlotte Van Oyen Witvliet, Pietro Pietrini, and Andrea J. Miller, "Forgiveness and Health," *Journal of Behavioral Medicine* 30 (2007): 291–302.
2. Robert M. Sapolsky, *Why Zebras Don't Get Ulcers: A Guide to Stress, Stress-Related Diseases, and Coping* (New York: W. H. Freeman, 1995).
3. Jon R. Webb, Elizabeth A. R. Robinson, Kirk J. Brower, and Robert A. Zucker, "Forgiveness and Alcohol Problems among People Entering Substance Abuse Treatment," *Journal of Addictive Diseases* 25 (2006): 55–67.
4. Benjamin A. Tabak, Michael E. McCullough, Angela Szeto, Armando J. Mendez, and Philip M. McCabe, "Oxytocin Indexes

Relational Distress Following Interpersonal Harms in Women," *Psychoneuroendocrinology* 36 (2011): 115–22.

5. John Maltby, Ann Macaskill, and Liza Day, "Failure to Forgive Self and Others: A Replication and Extension of the Relationship between Forgiveness, Personality, Social Desirability and General Health," *Personality and Individual Differences* 30 (2001): 881–85.
6. Barbara L. Fredrickson, *Positivity: Top-Notch Research Reveals the 3-to-1 Ratio That Will Change Your Life* (New York: Three Rivers, 2009).
7. Maltby, Macaskill, and Day, "Failure to Forgive Self and Others," 881–85.
8. Lois C. Friedman, et al., "Attribution of Blame, Self-forgiving Attitude and Psychological Adjustment in Women with Breast Cancer," *Journal of Behavioral Medicine* 30 (2007): 351–57; also, Catherine Romero, et al., "Self-forgiveness, Spirituality, and Psychological Adjustment in Women with Breast Cancer," *Journal of Behavioral Medicine* 29 (2006): 29–36.

Chapter 6

1. Corrie ten Boom, *Tramp for the Lord,* with Jamie Buckingham (New York: Jove Books, 2008), 85–88. Originally published 1974 by Fleming H. Revell.
2. The institute is now known as Richmont Graduate University.
3. Paul A. Mauger, et al., "The Measurement of Forgiveness: Preliminary Research," *Journal of Psychology and Christianity* 11 (1992): 170–80.
4. For a review, see Judith H. Hall and Frank D. Fincham, "Self-forgiveness: The Stepchild of Forgiveness Research," *Journal of Social and Clinical Psychology,* 24 (2005): For a good study, see Judith H. Hall and Frank D. Fincham, "The Temporal Course of Self-forgiveness," *Journal of Social and Clinical Psychology* 27 (2008): 174–202.

5. For a review, see Etienne Mullet, Félix Neto, and Sheila Rivière, "Personality and Its Effects on Resentment, Revenge, Forgiveness, and Self-Forgiveness," in *Handbook of Forgiveness,* ed. Everett L. Worthington Jr., (New York: Routledge, 2005), 159–82.
6. Louise Barber, John Maltby, and Ann Macaskill, "Angry Memories and Thoughts of Revenge: The Relationship between Forgiveness and Anger Rumination," *Personality and Individual Differences* 39 (2005): 253–62; Ann Macaskill, John Maltby, and Liza Day, "Forgiveness of Self and Others and Emotional Empathy," *Journal of Social Psychology* 142 (2002): 663–65; John Maltby, Ann Macaskill, and Liza Day, "Failure to Forgive Self and Others: A Replication and Extension of the Relationship between Forgiveness, Personality, Social Desirability and General Health," *Personality and Individual Differences* 30 (2001): 881–85. See also, Liza Day and John Maltby, "Forgiveness and Social Loneliness," *Journal of Psychology: Interdisciplinary and Applied* 139 (2005): 553–55.
7. Scott R. Ross, Matthew J. Hertenstein, and Thomas A. Wrobel, "Maladaptive Correlates of the Failure to Forgive Self and Others: Further Evidence for a Two-component Model of Forgiveness," *Journal of Personality Assessment* 88 (2007): 158–67; Scott R. Ross, et al., "A Personological Examination of Self and Other-forgiveness in the Five Factor Model," *Journal of Personality Assessment* 82 (2004): 207–14.
8. Barber, Maltby, and Macaskill, "Angry Memories and Thoughts of Revenge," 253–62; Macaskill, Maltby, and Day, "Forgiveness of Self and Others and Emotional Empathy," 663–65; Maltby, Macaskill, and Day, "Failure to Forgive Self and Others," 881–85. See also, Day and Maltby, "Forgiveness and Social Loneliness," 553–55.
9. Linda S. Mintle, *Breaking Free from a Negative Self-Image: Finding God's True Reflection When Your Mirror Lies* (Lake Mary, FL: Siloam, 2002).

10. Everett L. Worthington Jr., *How to Help the Hurting: When Friends Face Problems with Self-Esteem, Self-Control, Fear, Depression, Loneliness* (Downers Grove, IL: InterVarsity Press, 1985).
11. Lewis B. Smedes, *Shame and Grace: Healing the Shame We Don't Deserve* (New York: Harper San Francisco, 1993), 81.
12. For a review, see Hall and Fincham, "Self-forgiveness," 621–37. For a good study, see Hall and Fincham, "The Temporal Course of Self-forgiveness," 174–202.
13. Robert D. Enright and Human Development Study Group, "Counseling within the Forgiveness Triad: On Forgiving, Receiving Forgiveness, and Self-forgiveness," *Counseling and Values* 40 (1996): 107–26.
14. For a review, see Hall and Fincham, "Self-forgiveness," 621–37. For a good study, see Hall and Fincham, "The Temporal Course of Self-forgiveness," 174–202.

Chapter 7

1. Charles W. Colson, *Born Again* (Grand Rapids, MI: Chosen Books, 1976; repr.; 2008), 123–29.
2. Lewis B. Smedes, *Forgive and Forget: Healing the Hurts We Don't Deserve* (New York: Pocket Books, 1984), 98.
3. Mickie L. Fisher and Julie J. Exline, "Self-forgiveness Versus Excusing: The Roles of Remorse, Effort, and Acceptance of Responsibility," *Self and Identity* 5 (2006): 127–46.
4. For more on this, see Everett L. Worthington Jr., *Forgiving and Reconciling: Bridges to Wholeness and Hope* (Downers Grove, IL: InterVarsity Press, 2003).

Chapter 8

1. Mickie L. Fisher and Julie J. Exline, "Self-forgiveness Versus Excusing: The Roles of Remorse, Effort, and Acceptance of Responsibility," *Self and Identity* 5 (2006): 127–46.

2. Our team has investigated humility in depth. See Don E. Davis, et al., "Relational Spirituality and Forgiveness: Development of the Spiritual Humility Scale (SHS)," *Journal of Psychology and Theology* 38 (2010): 91–100; Don E. Davis, Everett L. Worthington Jr., and Joshua N. Hook, "Relational Humility: A Review of Definitions and Measurement Strategies," *Journal of Positive Psychology* 5 (2010): 243–52; Don E. Davis, et al., "Humility as Personality Judgment: Conceptualization and Development of the Relational Humility Scale (RHS)," *Journal for Personality Assessment* 93 (2011): 225–34.
3. Charles W. Colson, *Born Again* (Grand Rapids, MI: Chosen Books, 2008), 240–41.
4. Colson, *Born Again,* 241–42.

Chapter 9

1. *Something's Gotta Give,* written and directed by Nancy Meyers, Columbia Pictures, 2003.
2. See Mickie L. Fisher and Julie J. Exline, "Self-forgiveness Versus Excusing: The Roles of Remorse, Effort, and Acceptance of Responsibility," *Self and Identity* 5 (2006): 127–46.
3. See Judith H. Hall and Frank D. Fincham, "Self-forgiveness: The Stepchild of Forgiveness Research," Journal of Social and Clinical Psychology 24 (2005): 621–37; Judith H. Hall and Frank D. Fincham, "The Temporal Course of Self-forgiveness," Journal of Social and Clinical Psychology 27 (2008): 174–202.

Chapter 10

1. Kim Phuc, "Address at the United States Vietnam War Memorial, Veterans Day 1996," November 11, 1996, www.gos.sbc.edu/p/phuc.html. For a fuller account, see Denise Chong, *The Girl in the Picture: the Story of Kim Phuc, the Photograph, and the Vietnam War* (New York: Penguin Books, 1999) and John Plummer and Kim Phuc, "The Power of Forgiveness," *Guideposts,* October 8, 1997.

2. See the website of the Kim Foundation: www.kimfoundation .com/modules/contentpage/index.php?file=story.htm&ma=10& subid=101/.
3. Bill Clinton, *My Life: The Presidential Years, Volume II* (New York: Vintage Books, 2004), 420–21.
4. Clinton, *My Life,* 457–58.
5. Everett L. Worthington Jr., *Forgiving and Reconciling: Bridges to Wholeness and Hope* (Downers Grove, IL: InterVarsity Press, 2003).

Chapter 11

1. See the full story in Genesis 27–33. The brothers' reconciliation is recorded in Genesis 32:1–33:15.
2. Stephanie L. Brown, et al., "Providing Social Support May Be More Beneficial than Receiving It: Results from a Prospective Study of Mortality," *Psychological Science* 14 no. 4 (2003): 320–27.
3. Barbara L. Fredrickson, et al., "Open Hearts Build Lives: Positive Emotions, Induced through Meditation, Build Consequential Personal Resources," *Journal of Personality and Social Psychology* 95 no. 5 (2008): 1045–62.

Chapter 12

1. After much searching, I was unable to find the original source of this quote by Paul Tillich. The following book is faithful to the idea expressed in the quote. Paul Tillich, *Love, Power, and Justice: Ontological Analyses and Ethical Applications* (Oxford: Oxford University Press, 1954).
2. Blaise Pascal, *Pensées and Other Writings,* ed. Anthony Levi, trans. Honor Levi (Oxford: Oxford University Press, 2008). Originally published posthumously in 1669.
3. Malcolm Muggeridge, *Confessions of a Twentieth-Century Pilgrim* (San Francisco: HarperCollins, 1988).

4. Aleksandr Solzhenitsyn, *The Gulag Archipelago* (New York: Harper Perennial Modern Classics, 2002), 312.

Chapter 13

1. Adam B. Cohen, "Religion and the Morality of Mentality," *Journal of Personality and Social Psychology* 81 (2001): 697–710.
2. American Law Institute, *Draft of a Model Penal Code* (Philadelphia: American Law Institute, 1962).
3. Reepicheep appears in C. S. Lewis, *Prince Caspian: The Return to Narnia* (New York: Harper Trophy, 2000). First published 1951 by Macmillan. The character also appears in C. S. Lewis, *Voyage of the Dawn Treader* (New York: HarperFestival, 2011). First published 1952 by Macmillan.
4. See Richard J. Foster and Gayle D. Beebe, *Longing for God: Seven Paths of Christian Devotion* (Downers Grove, IL: InterVarsity Press, 2009).
5. Roy F. Baumeister, Kathleen D. Vohs, and Diane M. Tice, "The Strength Model of Self-control," *Current Directions in Psychological Science* 16 (2007): 351–55.

Chapter 14

1. Jack W. Berry, et al., "Forgiveness, Vengeful Rumination, and Affective Traits," *Journal of Personality* 73 (2005): 1–43.
2. *The Dream Team*, directed by Howard Zieff, written by John Connolly and David Loucka, Universal Pictures, 1989.
3. Daniel M. Wegner, *White Bears and Other Unwanted Thoughts: Suppression, Obsession, and the Psychology of Mental Control* (New York: Guilford Press, 1994).

Chapter 15

1. Everett L. Worthington Jr., *A Just Forgiveness: Responsible Healing Without Excusing Injustice* (Downers Grove, IL: InterVarsity Press, 2009).

2. Everett L. Worthington Jr., *Forgiving and Reconciling: Bridges to Wholeness and Hope* (Downers Grove, IL: InterVarsity Press, 2003).

Chapter 16

1. Everett L. Worthington Jr., *Forgiving and Reconciling: Bridges to Wholeness and Hope* (Downers Grove, IL: InterVarsity Press, 2003).
2. John Paul Lederac, "Five Qualities of Practice in Support of Reconciliation Processes," in *Forgiveness and Reconciliation: Religion, Public Policy, and Conflict Transformation,* ed. Raymond G. Helmick and Rodney L. Petersen, (Radnor, PA: Templeton Foundation Press, 2001), 186.
3. Everett L. Worthington Jr., *Humility: The Quiet Virtue* (West Conshohocken, PA: Templeton Foundation Press, 2007).

Chapter 17

1. See Viktor E. Frankl, *Man's Search for Meaning: An Introduction to Logotherapy* (New York: Pocket Books, 1959: repr.; 1979). Excerpts and paraphrased summaries in this chapter are taken from pages 129–33.
2. Frankl, *Man's Search for Meaning,* 132.
3. Carl R. Rogers, *Client-centered Therapy* (Boston: Houghton-Mifflin, 1951).
4. For practical help in getting across a heart knowledge of God's faithfulness that we can trust, I love this book by Peter van Breemen. See Peter G. van Breemen, *The God Who Won't Let Go* (Notre Dame, IN: Ave Maria Press, 2001).

Chapter 18

1. Roy F. Baumeister, Ellen Bratslavsky, Catrin Finkenauer, and Kathleen Vohs, "Bad Is Stronger Than Good," *Review* of *General Psychology* 5 (2001): 323–70.

2. See John Mordechai Gottman, *What Predicts Divorce?* (Hillsdale, NJ: Lawrence Erlbaum Associates, 1994).
3. Barbara L. Fredrickson, *Positivity: Groundbreaking Research Reveals How to Embrace the Hidden Strength of Positive Emotions, Overcome Negativity, and Thrive* (New York: Crown Archetype, 2009). Fredrickson reports on research on business groups that was conducted by herself and colleague Marcial Losada.
4. Marcial F. Losada, "The Complex Dynamics of High Performance Teams," *Mathematical and Computer Modelling* 30 no. 9–10 (1999): 179–92.
5. Malcolm Gladwell, *The Tipping Point: How Little Things Can Make a Big Difference* (Boston: Back Bay Books, 2002).
6. After a diligent search, even to the extent of enlisting the aid of research librarians, I was not able to locate the original source of the quoted matter, which in multiple published and Internet references is attributed to William Temple, former Archbishop of Canterbury.
7. Attributed to Myra Brooks Welch, "The Touch of the Master's Hand." This poem exists in many forms—which becomes evident when one conducts an Internet search. After a diligent search, even to the extent of enlisting the aid of research librarians, I was not able to identify the original publishing data for this poem. I must conclude that the text is in the public domain. (The poem has been used as a song lyric. See the recordings of Dove-Award-winning singer Wayne Watson, for example. In that instance the melody is copyrighted, but not the lyrics.) In chapter 18 I quoted what might be called a contemporary USA version—using dollars instead of guineas, employing some modern contractions, and grouping the lines into four-line stanzas. The story of the poem's publication (again, reputedly) is as follows. In 1921 Myra Brooks heard a speaker and was so emotionally moved that she went home and wrote the poem in thirty minutes. She published it anonymously in a church bulletin. When its

popularity spread, it was attributed to Author Unknown. One night in the 1930s, after the poem was read in a group and attributed anonymously, a young man stood and said, "I know the author. It is my mother, Myra Welch." The story of this poet is that she knew personally what it meant to be battered and scarred. She suffered from severe arthritis and was forced to use a wheelchair. Myra Welch typed by holding a pencil, eraser-end down, and pecking out words, letter by letter, on her typewriter. Her poetic creation was the touch of her masterly, even though deformed, hand because she had experienced the redeeming touch of her—and our—Master's hand and she wanted to tell others.

Chapter 19

1. I am indebted to my son, Jonathan Worthington, for this insight.
2. *The Mission,* directed by Roland Joffé, written by Robert Bolt, Warner Brothers Pictures, 1986.
3. Peter van Breemen, *The God Who Won't Let Go* (Notre Dame, IN: Ave Maria Press, 2001), 47.
4. After a fruitless search, I have been unable to find the exact source of this quote. The following book captures Erwin Lutzer's meaning. Erwin W. Lutzer, *When You've Been Wronged: Moving from Bitterness to Forgiveness* (Chicago: Moody Publishers, 2007).
5. Breemen, *The God Who Won't Let Go,* 55.

Chapter 20

1. Immaculée Ilibagiza, *Left to Tell: Discovering God Amidst the Rwandan Holocaust,* with Steve Erwin (Carlsbad, CA: Hay House, 2007).